The Image of

Thomas Jefferson

in the Public Eye

Portraits for the People

1800-1809

Thomas Jefferson

Noble E. Cunningham, Jr.

The Image of Thomas Jefferson in the Public Eye

Portraits for the People

1800-1809

UNIVERSITY PRESS OF VIRGINIA

Charlottesville

This title is published with the support of
the Thomas Jefferson Memorial Foundation.

THE UNIVERSITY PRESS OF VIRGINIA

First published 1981

Library of Congress Cataloging in Publication Data
Cunningham, Noble E 1926–
The image of Thomas Jefferson in the public eye.

Includes index.
1. Jefferson, Thomas, Pres. U.S., 1743–1826—
Portraits, etc. I. Title
N7628.J4C86 769'.423'0973 80–22757
ISBN 0–8139–0821–3

Printed in the United States of America

TO

DUMAS MALONE

Preface

THERE IS WIDE ACQUAINTANCE TODAY WITH THE ARTISTIC treasures that have preserved the image of Thomas Jefferson. We are familiar with Houdon's incomparable bust of Jefferson, with the penetrating portraits by Rembrandt Peale and Gilbert Stuart, with the equally remarkable paintings by John Trumbull, and with other important life portraits. But relatively few of Jefferson's contemporaries saw these works, and the oil portraits that today provide our most vivid impressions of Jefferson were known to most of them only through engravings. In a republic where the profile of the head of state did not appear on coins, the public had no ready reference to the appearance of President Jefferson. Jefferson's profile did appear on two medals, but one of those was given only to chiefs of Indian tribes. What the ordinary person saw mostly were engraved prints, the merits of which varied considerably in capturing the images of the original portraits. The prints appeared separately and in books and periodicals; some of them were transferred onto pieces of Liverpool pottery — mainly pitchers and mugs — and some people may have gained their only impression of their president from these household items. There were only a few caricatures of President Jefferson — not as many as one would have suspected from the later flourishing of that art in the United States — and it is not at all clear how many people actually saw the caricatures that did appear. Silhouettes made from Houdon's bust were given away at Peale's Museum in Philadelphia, but if any of them have survived today, they have not been located. Although they may not have been deemed valuable enough for preservation, the contemporary demand for them was high.

The likenesses of Jefferson reproduced on the following pages enable the viewer to see Jefferson as he was seen by his contemporaries at the time of his presidency. The focus is on his presidential years and the preceding election year, because that was the period of the public's most intense interest in Jefferson and because it was a time of major artistic accomplishment in Jefferson portraiture and flourishing production of derivative portraits for the people. The original portraits that were the sources for the popular images of Jefferson, but which were seen by only a limited number of people, have been reproduced at the end of the book for reference. They have been separated from their derivatives in order to provide as far as possible an opportunity to appreciate the image that was available to the ordinary person.

I have attempted to make the study useful to scholars by reproducing prints that are rarely seen outside specialized museum collections and rare book rooms and by tracing their origins and derivations. I have also sought to discover the contemporary circumstances surrounding the making and the distribution of the prints and other likenesses. I have given most attention to those prints that were directed to the largest possible public audience. While there may be other likenesses that belong to this period, I have tried to be comprehensive; but I have included in the catalogue only those items that can be clearly documented as having been produced or seen by Jefferson's contemporaries during the period from 1800 to 1809. It is expected that the catalogue, as the first such venture in Jefferson iconography, will not prove to be definitive.

The present study shows that much of what Jefferson's contemporaries saw was not artistically very good — particularly during the first years of his presidency — and we may suspect that many of the people who twice elected Jefferson to the presidency did not have a very clear impression of what he looked like. But his portrait and other images were more widely distributed and circulated than previously recognized. The likenesses of Jefferson that were offered to the public not only reflect the interest in the man and the high office he held but also display the state of the arts in the young nation.

We have very little evidence of the impressions that the engraved prints and other contemporary images of President Jefferson made on the people who saw them, and we cannot say how these visual experiences altered their perceptions of him. But by looking at what the people saw, the viewer today can share a common experience with Jefferson's contemporaries and in his or her own eye form an impression of the image seen in an earlier age.

For support of the research for this book, I am indebted to the American Philosophical Society for a Penrose Fund Grant and to the Research Council of the University of Missouri, Columbia, for continuing grants over several years; I have also benefited as a recipient of a University of Missouri, Columbia, Chancellor's Award for Outstanding Research. For supporting the publication of the work, I am grateful to the Thomas Jefferson Memorial Foundation, Monticello, and its director, James A. Bear, Jr. For their efficient typing of the manuscript, I want to thank Phyllis Dussel and Ida Mae Wolff of the staff of the Department of History, University of Missouri, Columbia.

Among the many persons who have aided me in my work on this book, I particularly want to acknowledge the assistance of the following: Silvio A. Bedini, Smithsonian Institution; Julian P. Boyd, Princeton University; Herbert Collins, Smithsonian Institution; Harold Jefferson Coolidge, Beverly, Massachusetts; Anne Edwards, Ellis Library, University of Missouri; Ann Farnam, Essex Institute; Charles L. Granquist, Thomas Jefferson Memorial Foundation, Monticello; Steven H. Hochman, University of Virginia; David Kiehl, Metropolitan Museum of Art; David Meschutt, Frick Art Reference Library; Ellen G. Miles, National

Portrait Gallery; J. Jefferson Miller II, Smithsonian Institution; M. Bonner Mitchell, University of Missouri; Michael R. Parkinson, City Art Gallery, Manchester, England; Michael F. Plunkett, University of Virginia Library; E. P. Richardson, American Philosophical Society; Elizabeth E. Roth, New York Public Library; William Runge, McGregor Library, University of Virginia; Mattie U. Russell, Perkins Library, Duke University; Helen Sanger, Frick Art Reference Library; Alan Smith, Manchester, England; Wilcomb Washburn, Smithsonian Institution.

In my research and in assembling the materials for the reproductions in this book, I have drawn upon the resources of a large number of institutions, and I am obligated to them and their staffs for making available their holdings and providing helpful assistance. These include: American Antiquarian Society; American Numismatic Society; American Philosophical Society; Atwater Kent Museum; Boston Museum of Fine Arts; Bowdoin College Museum of Art; City Art Gallery, Manchester, England; Dedham Historical Society; Duke University Library; Essex Institute; Fogg Art Museum, Harvard University; Free Library of Philadelphia; Frick Art Reference Library; Historical Society of Pennsylvania; Houghton Library, Harvard University; Lafayette College; Library Company of Philadelphia; Library of Congress; Massachusetts Historical Society; Metropolitan Museum of Art; National Museum of History and Technology, Smithsonian Institution; National Portrait Gallery, Smithsonian Institution; New-York Historical Society; New York Public Library; Peabody Museum of Salem; Princeton University Library; Thomas Jefferson Memorial Foundation, Monticello; University of Missouri Library; University of Virginia Library; Virginia Historical Society; Virginia State Library; The White House; Worcester Art Museum; and Yale University Art Gallery.

NOBLE E. CUNNINGHAM, JR.

University of Missouri
Columbia

Contents

Illustrations

Illustrations

The Image of
Thomas Jefferson
in the Public Eye

Portraits for the People

1800-1809

CHAPTER I

First Impressions

THOMAS JEFFERSON IS A TALL MAN, SAY SIX FEET, AND thin. His hair which has been red is now grey and is worn in negligent disorder, though not ungracefully. His complexion is ruddy and his eyes (a hazel) very animated." Thus was Jefferson seen by the artist William Dunlap, who had just met the president when he recorded this description in February 1806.[1] Only a few days earlier Dunlap had been at the James Madisons' house in Washington, where he had seen Gilbert Stuart's recent portrait of the president, and after Mrs. Madison loaned him the painting to copy, he wrote excitedly to his wife that his head was "full of Jeffersons."[2] Artists were not the only persons interested in what Jefferson looked like; numerous visitors to Washington and many

[1]Dunlap to his wife, Feb. 25, 1806, *Diary of William Dunlap (1766–1839)*, 3 vols. (New York, 1930), 2: 388. Punctuation and spelling have been modernized.

[2]Feb. 19, 20, 1806, ibid., 2:387, 388. The evidence supplied by Dunlap that Madison's replica of Stuart's 1805 life portrait of Jefferson had been completed and was in Madison's possession as early as 1806 is important documentation relating to Stuart's work that has been previously overlooked. Jefferson's statement in 1814 that a

members of Congress recorded their impressions of Jefferson's appearance. Some observers spent more time describing his clothes than his features, but they all reflected an interest in the physical appearance of a man whose ideas and political principles were clearer in many people's eyes than his face. Most observers commented on Jefferson's height; many called attention to his "red freckled face and grey neglected hair." One dinner guest during the last year of his presidency observed surprisingly that "there is scarce a wrinkle on his brow." With the stylized costumes that embellished their portraits, no artist caught the casualness of Jefferson's dress that was so frequently noticed. "He was drest, or rather *undrest*," wrote Senator William Plumer upon meeting the president in 1802, "with an old brown coat, red waistcoat, old corduroy small clothes, much soiled — woolen hose — and slippers without heels."[3] Frances Few, a Washington visitor, reported that Jefferson wore to dinner in 1808 an old fringed dimity jacket that he had brought from France, where he had not been for nearly twenty

copy of this portrait was in Madison's possession has generally been cited as the earliest reference to the Madison replica. See Fiske Kimball, "The Life Portraits of Jefferson and Their Replicas," American Philosophical Society, *Proceedings* 78 (1944): 516; and Alfred L. Bush, "The Life Portraits of Thomas Jefferson," in William Howard Adams, ed., *Jefferson and the Arts: An Extended View* (Washington, D.C., 1976), p. 74.

Dunlap completed a miniature of Stuart's painting, but its existence today is unknown (Dunlap to his wife, Feb. 28, 1806, *Diary of William Dunlap*, 2:393; William Dunlap, *A History of the Rise and Progress of the Arts of Design in the United States* [1834], ed. Frank W. Bayley and Charles E. Goodspeed, 3 vols. [Boston, 1918], 1: 322).

[3]Richard Beale Davis, ed., *Jeffersonian America: Notes on the United States of America Collected in the Years 1805–6–7 and 11–12 by Sir Augustus John Foster, Bart.* (San Marino, Calif., 1954), p. 10; Frances Few, Oct. 1808, Noble E. Cunningham, Jr., ed., "The Diary of Frances Few," *Journal of Southern History* 29 (1963): 350; Plumer to Jeremiah Smith, Dec. 9, 1802, William Plumer Papers, Library of Congress.

years. Senator Samuel Latham Mitchill in recording his first impressions of Jefferson observed: "He is tall in stature and rather spare in flesh. His dress and manners are very plain. He is grave or rather sedate; but without any tincture of pomp, ostentation or pride. And occasionally can smile."[4] The numerous descriptions of Jefferson in private letters and journals provide a good picture of his appearance, but the general public in Jefferson's day did not have access to the files that historians can consult today. Most contemporaries had to rely on an artist's skills — and sometimes the work of an unskilled engraver — in forming their visual images of Thomas Jefferson.

Until Jefferson became a candidate for the presidency in 1800, the public outside his home state of Virginia and the national capital at Philadelphia had had little opportunity to form an impression of what he looked like. The first public exhibition of a likeness of Jefferson was in Paris at the Salon of 1789, when Jean-Antoine Houdon's plaster bust (Appendix, plate I) was displayed in the summer exhibition of the Royal Academy of Painting and Sculpture.[5] In 1793, some three years after Jefferson returned to the United States, he gave one of the original Houdon busts to David Rittenhouse in Philadelphia, where it became known to others and in 1811 was presented to the American Philosophical Society.[6] It was in Paris that Jefferson sat for John Trumbull, who painted his

[4]Cunningham, ed., "Diary of Frances Few," p. 350; Mitchill to his wife, Jan. 10, 1802, Samuel Latham Mitchill Papers, Museum of the City of New York. For another description, see Samuel Taggart to the Rev. John Taylor, Jan 13, 1804, George H. Haynes, ed., "Letters of Samuel Taggart, Representative in Congress, 1803–1814," American Antiquarian Society, *Proceedings*, new ser., 33 (1923): 124–25.

[5]Bush, "Life Portraits of Jefferson," p. 17; Kimball, "Life Portraits of Jefferson," p. 505; Howard C. Rice, Jr., *Thomas Jefferson's Paris* (Princeton, N.J., 1976), p. 33.

[6]Brooke Hindle, *David Rittenhouse* (Princeton, N.J., 1964), p. 336; *A Catalogue of Portraits and Other Works of Art in the Possession of the American Philosophical Society* (Philadelphia, 1961), p. 53.

portrait in the original small *Declaration of Independence*. This now widely known painting, however, remained in Trumbull's possession until 1832, and he did not paint the life-size version that hangs in the rotunda of the United States Capitol until 1818. The earliest engraving of the *Declaration*, by Asher Brown Durand, was published in 1823. Although Trumbull copied three miniatures of Jefferson from the *Declaration* soon after the original was painted, the public had access to none of these.[7] In Paris Jefferson also sat in 1789 for a drawing by Edmé Quenedey employing the physiognotrace invented by his partner, Gilles-Louis Chrétien, who then engraved Quenedey's delineation. Jefferson received twelve engravings and the plate from which they were taken, but none of the prints is known to have survived. Later, probably about 1801, Quenedey reengraved the portrait, but only three examples are known, and no record of their distribution has been found.[8] The American public almost certainly saw none of these.

The first public display in the United States of a portrait of Jefferson was in Peale's Museum in Philadelphia. In 1791 Jefferson, then secretary of state, sat for Charles Willson Peale, who

[7]Kimball, "Life Portraits of Jefferson," pp. 501, 503; Bush, "Life Portraits of Jefferson," pp. 25–26; Theodore Sizer, *The Works of Colonel John Trumbull: Artist of the American Revolution* (rev. ed., New Haven, 1967), p. 96, and notes under fig. 158; Theodore Sizer, ed., *The Autobiography of Colonel John Trumbull: Patriot-Artist, 1756–1843* (New Haven, 1953), pp. 320–21.

[8]Bush, "Life Portraits of Jefferson," pp. 26–29; René Hennequin, *Avant les Photographies: Les Portraits au Physionotrace, Gravés de 1788 à 1830* (Troyes, 1932), pp. 59–60; Howard C. Rice, Jr., "A 'New' Likeness of Thomas Jefferson," *William and Mary Quarterly*, 3d ser., 6 (1949): 84–89; Julian P. Boyd, ed., *The Papers of Thomas Jefferson* (Princeton, N.J., 1950—), 14: xli-xliv. Quenedey's sketch of the physiognotrace and an explanation of its operation can be found in Howard C. Rice, Jr., "Saint-Mémin's Portrait of Jefferson," *Princeton University Library Chronicle* 20 (1959): 183, 191–92. See also Rice, *Jefferson's Paris*, p. 17.

added his portrait to the gallery of distinguished Americans on exhibit in the museum (Appendix, plate II). The work was listed in the gallery catalogue in 1795, shortly after the removal of Peale's collection to Philosophical Hall, and in 1802 it went on display in Peale's expanded museum on the upper floor of the Pennsylvania State House (Independence Hall), where it remained for the next quarter of a century.[9] The first print of an engraving of Jefferson to be seen by the public was taken from this portrait. First engraved in 1795 by William Birch, this work is not known to have been published except for a proof print. The only record located relating to Birch's engraving is an entry in a catalogue of the 1795 exhibition of the Columbianum, a newly organized academy of arts in Philadelphia, held in the Senate chamber of the Pennsylvania State House. Among the works exhibited by William Birch, enamel painter and engraver, was "a proof print done from a portrait of Mr. Jefferson in Peale's Museum." Birch offered it as a specimen of a series of twenty-five prints to be made from portraits in Peale's collection and opened a subscription book. Apparently his plan did not attract sufficient interest and support to be pursued, and nothing is known of the fate of his engraved plate of Jefferson. No print from it is known to have survived.[10]

The Gentleman's Political Pocket Almanac, for the Year 1797, published in New York by Charles Smith, contained portraits of Jefferson and Madison, but neither the artist nor the engraver was

[9] Bush, "Life Portraits of Jefferson," p. 38; [Charles Willson Peale], *An Historical Catalogue of Peale's Collection of Paintings* (Philadelphia, 1795), p. 16; Charles Coleman Sellers, *Portraits and Miniatures of Charles Willson Peale* (Philadelphia, 1952), pp. 17, 111; Charles Coleman Sellers, *Charles Willson Peale*, 2 vols. (Philadelphia, 1947), 2: 60–61, 152–53;

[10] *The Exhibition of the Columbianum, or American Academy of Painting, Sculpture, Architecture, &c. Established at Philadelphia, 1795* (Philadelphia, 1795), American Philosophical Society; *Aurora* (Philadelphia), May 1, June 26, 1795; Bush, "Life Portraits of Jefferson," p. 39.

identified; and the source of the portrait of Jefferson is not clear.[11] The most important use of this image came after Jefferson's election as president when it appeared in James Hardie's *The New Universal Biographical Dictionary* (see fig. 2). Meanwhile, as the election of 1800 approached, various new engravings of Jefferson were prepared. One of the first of these to reach the public appeared in Philadelphia early in 1800. On January 11, the Philadelphia *Aurora* printed the following advertisement:

> JUST PUBLISHED,
> AND TO BE HAD AT THE OFFICE OF
> THE AURORA.
> At D. Kennedy's corner of 7th and Market-Street, and of Wm. Y. Birch, No. 17, South second-street, a portrait of the Hon. Thomas Jefferson, engraved by Akin and Harrison, jun. from the picture now in the Museum painted by C. W. Peale.
> January 11.

This print (fig. 1) by James Akin and William Harrison, Jr., is a reasonably faithful engraving of Peale's 1791 portrait, showing Jefferson as secretary of state at age forty-eight. When the print appeared, Jefferson was approaching fifty-seven and, as identified in the inscription, was vice-president of the United States. The public thus saw a younger man than the candidate who was being widely promoted for the presidency when Akin and Harrison published their print. The engravers, however, made no attempt to suggest a current likeness, indicating on the print that the portrait had been painted by C. W. Peale in 1791. An interesting aspect of the inscription is the designation of Jefferson not only as vice-president but also as president of the American Philosophical Society — an office in which he had been installed on March 3, 1797, the evening before he became vice-president.[12] Although it is not

[11] See National Portrait Gallery, Smithsonian Institution, *Permanent Collection Illustrated Checklist*, comp. Linda T. Neumaier (Washington, D.C., 1978), p. 74.

[12] Dumas Malone, *Jefferson and the Ordeal of Liberty* (Boston, 1962), pp. 340–41.

Fig. 1. Thomas Jefferson. Engraving by James Akin and William Harrison, Jr., Philadelphia, January 10, 1800

known how widely this print was sold, it was one of the earliest opportunities that the public at large had to see Jefferson's portrait.

About the same time that Akin and Harrison were promoting their print in Philadelphia, James Sharples in New York was advertising "Polygraphick Copies" of his original portrait of Jefferson — one of "upwards of 200 original paintings of the most celebrated personages in the United States" that he claimed made up his collection. He promised to make "Polygraphick Copies" from any of his portraits when ten orders were placed and announced that he had already completed copies of the portraits of eight leading figures. Among them was Jefferson. Sharples offered the profiles for $2.50 each.[13] Whether because of the fragile nature of the profiles or because of poor sales, none of Sharples's polygraphic copies is known to have survived, or, if so, it has not been identified.[14]

Regardless of whether they purchased copies, numerous Americans did have opportunities to see Sharples's original drawings — made in pastel crayons with the aid of a physiognotrace — in public exhibitions, such as the month-long display in New York during July 1798, at 104 Broadway, opposite Trinity Church. Admission was one quarter dollar.[15] Jefferson's portrait (Appendix, plate III) was almost certainly among those on exhibit, for all evi-

[13] Advertisement in the *Commercial Advertiser* (New York), Jan. 1, 1800, in Rita Susswein Gottesman, *The Arts and Crafts in New York, 1800–1804: Advertisements and News Items from New York City Newspapers* (New York, 1965), p. 15. The advertisement also appeared in the *Daily Advertiser* (New York), Jan. 17, 1800.

[14] No mention of polygraphic copies has been found in any work on Sharples, including the most extensive study that has appeared: Katharine McCook Knox, *The Sharples, Their Portraits of George Washington and His Contemporaries: A Diary and an Account of the Life and Work of James Sharples and His Family in England and America* (New Haven, 1930).

[15] Advertisement in the *Daily Advertiser*, July 17, 1798, in Rita Susswein Gottesman, *The Arts and Crafts in New York, 1777–1799: Advertisements and News Items from New York City Newspapers* (New York, 1954), p. 19.

dence indicates that Sharples had drawn Jefferson in Philadelphia soon after Jefferson became vice-president in 1797.[16] Others may have seen the portrait as Sharples and his family traveled around the country in a specially designed carriage. He drew "immense numbers" of portraits, said William Dunlap (who knew him well), "generally *en profile*, and, when so, strikingly like."[17] Although only two of Sharples's profiles of Jefferson are known today,[18] an indeterminate number of Americans may have gained their first impression of Jefferson's features from the likeness by Sharples.

Others may have gained their first impression from the print included in James Hardie's *The New Universal Biographical Dictionary*, which began publication in New York in 1801.[19] An advertisement dated June 11, 1801, appearing in the New York *American Citizen*, announced the publication that day of the second number of Hardie's work and sought subscribers with the inducement that "*This number is embellished with a Portrait of* THOMAS JEFFERSON, *President of the United States*." The notice also outlined the publication plans for the projected four-volume work, indicating that it would consist of thirty-two numbers, "each containing sixty four pages, embellished with a likeness of some distinguished American." "A number shall be delivered once a fortnight, or oftener, if possible, till the whole is completed. Price 25 cents,

[16] Bush, "Life Portraits of Jefferson," p. 44. The portrait and a copy, both of which can be traced to the collection in the hands of the Sharples family, survive (ibid., p. 42). See note 18 below.

[17] Dunlap also reported that "his price for the profile was $15; and for the full face (never so good) $20" (Dunlap, *History . . . of the Arts of Design*, 2: 205). Dunlap made no reference to polygraphic copies.

[18] One is in Independence Hall, Philadelphia, and the other, in the City Art Gallery, Bristol, Eng. Bush tentatively identified the example in Bristol as the original life portrait and the profile in Philadelphia as a copy ("Life Portraits of Jefferson," pp. 42–45).

[19] James Hardie, *The New Universal Biographical Dictionary, and American Remembrancer of Departed Merit . . .* , 4 vols. (New York, 1801–5).

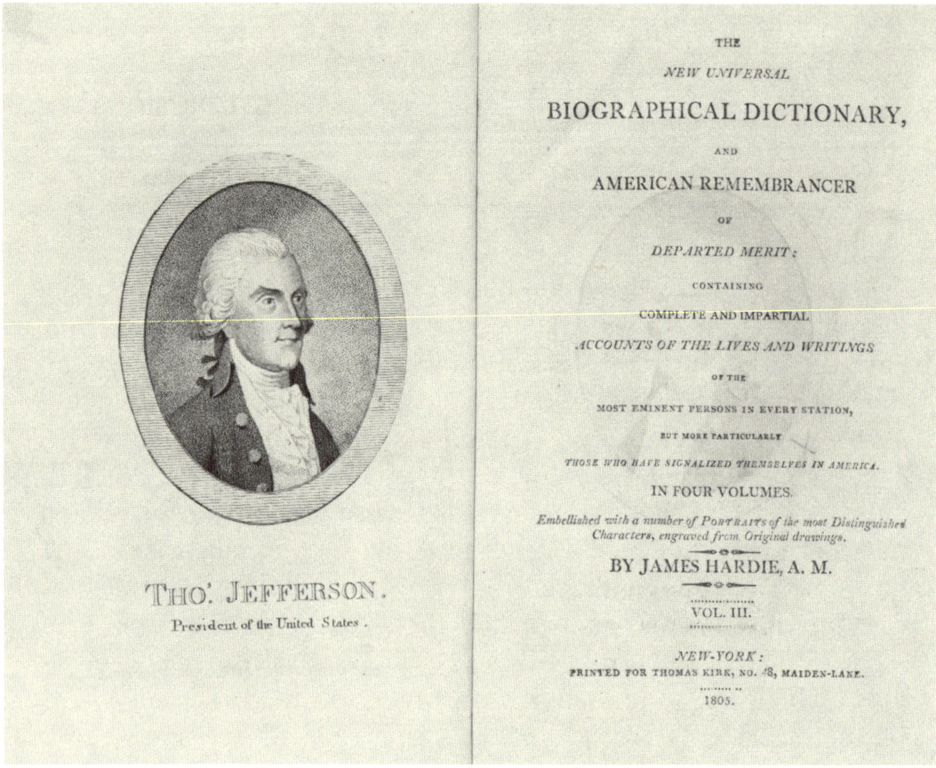

Fig. 2. James Hardie's New Universal Biographical Dictionary, *New York, 1805. Frontispiece and title page of volume 3. Engraving by unknown artist*

payable on delivery."[20] Thus, for twenty-five cents a purchaser could obtain, along with a section of Hardie's *Biographical Dictionary*, a portrait of Jefferson—relatively easy public access to a likeness of the recently installed president, though it was not a very accurate or current portrait, and the source of the portrait was never identified. In the 1805 edition of Hardie's work, the same engraving of Jefferson that appeared in 1801 was published as the frontispiece of the third volume (fig. 2). Hardie's publication had the potential for widespread distribution and may have furnished many Americans with an impression of a younger and more dashing man than the stern figure of Jefferson that appeared in some other publications during the election of 1800 and the early months of his presidency.

[20]*American Citizen*, June 30, 1801. In bound volumes of Hardie's work, the engraving of Jefferson appears facing p. 65 in the 1801 edition.

CHAPTER II

The Brief Vogue of Edward Savage

WITH THE PUBLIC'S INCREASING INTEREST IN JEFFERSON as the Republican party candidate for president in 1800, portrait painters sought him out for sittings, and engravers and printers became increasingly active in providing the public with prints showing representations of his likeness. During 1800 Jefferson sat for three portrait painters, at least two of whom produced likenesses that became known to the public through the copies — and not infrequently the distortions — of engravers. Although the precise dates for all sittings cannot be established, it was most likely between Jefferson's arrival in Philadelphia in late December 1799 and his departure for Monticello in mid-May 1800 that he sat for Rembrandt Peale, gifted son of Charles Willson Peale, for Edward Savage, less talented but widely copied, and for Gilbert Stuart, the acknowledged master of American portraiture.[1] Stuart's 1800 life portrait of Jefferson is not known to survive today, and there is no reliable evidence that it was ever engraved.[2] The portrait by Peale, known today as one of the most important representations of Jeffer-

[1] Bush, "Life Portraits of Jefferson," pp. 55, 60, 62.

[2] See pp. 31–45, 88 below.

son ever painted, was engraved soon after its completion and became the leading public image of Jefferson during the early years of his presidency. The portrait by Savage painted in 1800 is known today only through engravings — the medium in which the public mainly saw it in the early 1800s.

Before being eclipsed by Peale's superior work, the image supplied by Savage enjoyed a brief but widespread popularity. Whether visitors to Savage's "New Exhibition Gallery of Paintings" at his painting rooms in Philadelphia in 1800 saw the original painting is unknown, though it may have been among his exhibition of "original American Historical Paintings taken from the most interesting subjects."[3] It is certain that New Yorkers saw the portrait after Savage moved to New York in 1801 and opened the Columbian Gallery "containing a large collection of Ancient and Modern Paintings, Prints, and Sculpture." Informing the public in a newspaper advertisement that "to this collection Mr. Savage has added several pieces of his own," Savage did not mention his Jefferson portrait. However, the exhibition at the Columbian Gallery in 1802 — New York's first major art show — was reviewed in the *Morning Chronicle* by the city's first art critic, who listed: "No. 95. A portrait of the President of the United States, by Savage." The critic's assessment was that "this artist is certainly happy in taking strong likenesses, and this perhaps is the chief duo'vre [*sic*] of his pencil."[4]

[3]*Aurora*, Apr. 4, 1800, in Alfred Coxe Prime, ed., *The Arts and Crafts in Philadelphia, Maryland, and South Carolina, 1786–1800: Gleanings from Newspapers* (The Walpole Society, 1932), p. 34; Bush, "Life Portraits of Jefferson," p. 60.

[4]*New York Gazette and General Advertiser*, May 11, 1802, in I. N. Phelps Stokes, *The Iconography of Manhattan Island*, 6 vols. (New York, 1915–28), 5: 1391; Gottesman, *Arts and Crafts in New York, 1800–1804*, p. xi; *Morning Chronicle* (New York), Jan. 3, 1803, ibid., p. 36. The series of reviews began on Nov. 5, 1802, and concluded on Jan. 3, 1803.

If it is assumed that Savage's portrait was still on exhibit at the Columbian Gallery on January 3, 1803, when this review appeared, it seems unlikely that the painting was destroyed by fire in the Columbian Museum in Boston on the evening of January 15, 1803, as has commonly been surmised.[5] The Columbian Museum in Boston, established by Daniel Bowen in 1795, did contain among its paintings a portrait of Jefferson, but no record has been located to indicate that it was Savage's. Furthermore, Savage himself was still operating his gallery in New York in January 1803, and in February 1803 in a letter to Jefferson he described the expansion of his museum in New York in terms that he almost certainly would not have used had he recently shipped part of his collection to Boston.[6] He also solicited the president's support for his plans to publish an engraved print of the signing of the Declaration of Independence, and soon thereafter he was advertising plans for the print in New York newspapers. "Striking likenesses of the principal characters who composed the Congress of that day, will be introduced," he declared, "and the Print will contain from thirty to forty portraits, taken from life. Among those already in possession of the Artist, are . . . Thomas Jefferson. . . ." Whether Savage meant that these portraits had been drawn on his canvas of the signing or as separate portraits is unclear, but in any case it seems unlikely that he would not have had his portrait of Jefferson in his possession at the time he made this announcement two months after the fire in Boston. As for the announced engraving of the signing, though Savage had assured Jefferson that he intended to finish it as soon as possible and Jefferson had readily agreed to

[5] Bush, "Life Portraits of Jefferson," p. 60; Andrew Oliver, *Portraits of John and Abigail Adams* (Cambridge, Mass., 1967), p. 113.

[6] Sketch of the Columbian Museum, Boston, in *The Monthly Anthology and Boston Review* 1 (Jan. 1804): 143; *Morning Chronicle*, Jan. 2, 1803, in Gottesman, *Arts and Crafts in New York, 1800–1804*, p. 448; Savage to Jefferson, Feb. 7, 1803, Thomas Jefferson Papers, Lib. Cong.

become a subscriber, it remained uncompleted at the time of Savage's death in 1817.[7]

Whatever happened to Savage's original portrait of Jefferson, most people saw not that likeness but the mezzotint that Savage published in Philadelphia, June 1, 1800, and signed as both painter and engraver (fig. 3).[8] The engraving is less successful in capturing the likeness of Jefferson than Rembrandt Peale's portrait, but Savage's image was widely copied at the beginning of Jefferson's presidency. That was no doubt due partly to the availability of the mezzotint at a time when engravers and publishers were looking for portraits of the recently elected president of the United States with which to embellish their works. Although little known today, the Savage image of Jefferson must have been widely seen by his contemporaries.

During the year 1801 five separate editions of Jefferson's *Notes on the State of Virginia*, first printed in Paris in 1785, were published, and all contain, in at least some copies, portraits of Jefferson as frontispieces. None of the previous editions of Jefferson's book had included a portrait of the author. Of these five editions, the Savage image, grossly distorted by engravers, appears in four.[9]

[7] Advertisement in *Chronicle Express* (New York), Mar. 17, 1803, in Gottesman, *Arts and Crafts in New York, 1800–1804*, pp. 60–62; Savage to Jefferson, Feb. 7, 1803, Jefferson to Savage, Mar. 4, 1803, Jefferson Papers, Lib. Cong.; Oliver, *Portraits of John and Abigail Adams*, p. 112.

[8] The engraving is signed "E Savage Pinx & sc." Savage's engraving of the plate has been questioned, and it has been argued that John Wesley Jarvis and David Edwin, who worked for Savage, did much of the engraving. The case against Savage is hearsay and circumstantial, but Savage's engravings may not have been entirely his own work (Harold E. Dickson, "The Case against Savage," *American Collector* 14 [1946]: 6–7, 17).

[9] Coolie Verner, *A Further Checklist of the Separate Editions of Jefferson's Notes on the State of Virginia* (Charlottesville, Va., 1950), pp. 13–17. Verner misidentified these engravings as "after the Rem-

Fig. 3. Thomas Jefferson. Mezzotint by Edward Savage, Philadelphia, June 1, 1800

---

brandt Peale portrait" in "The Maps and Plates Appearing with the Several Editions of Mr. Jefferson's 'Notes on the State of Virginia,'" *Virginia Magazine of History and Biography* 59 (1951): 31–32.

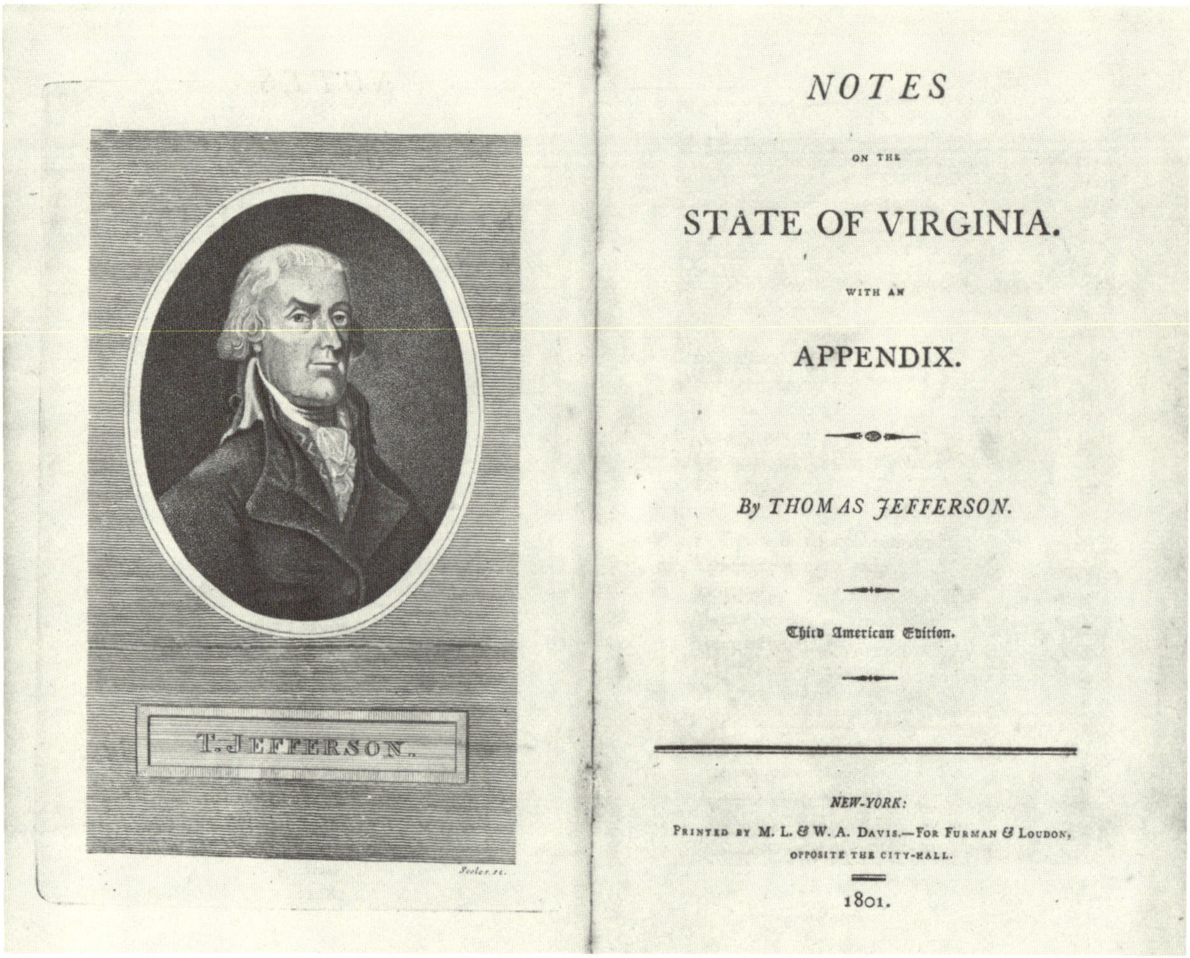

Fig. 4. Jefferson's Notes on the State of Virginia, *New York, 1801. Frontispiece and title page. Engraving by John Scoles*

Three editions — the Newark 1801 edition and two editions published in New York in 1801 — contain the same frontispiece engraved by John Scoles and signed "Scoles, sc." (fig. 4).[10] All appear

[10] Thomas Jefferson, *Notes on the State of Virginia* (3d American ed., Newark, N.J.: Pennington & Gould, 1801); Thomas Jefferson, *Notes on the State of Virginia* (3d American ed., New York: M. L. & W. A. Davis, for Furman & Loudon, 1801); Thomas Jefferson, *Notes on the State of Virginia* (4th American ed., New York: T. B. Jansen & Co. & G. Jansen & Co., 1801). The best collection of Jefferson's *Notes on the State of Virginia*, containing all of the various editions, is in the McGregor Library of the University of Virginia, Charlottesville.

to have been printed from the same plate. The fourth 1801 edition of Jefferson's *Notes on Virginia* to contain the Savage image was published in Boston (fig. 5).[11] While similar to the Scoles engraving, the print in the Boston edition was engraved by Enoch G. Gridley. Not all copies contain a signed state of the engraving, but the unsigned prints are otherwise identical to those that included "Gridley sc." inscribed in very small lettering immediately under the portrait.[12]

It is impossible to determine how many copies of Jefferson's *Notes on Virginia* were sold during 1801, but the number of printers and booksellers involved in publishing and selling the work and the numerous copies that survive today suggest a wide distribution. Nine New England bookdealers are listed on the title page of the Boston 1801 edition. Some dealers clearly used the portrait of Jefferson as a selling point. Furman and Loudon published advertisements for their New York 1801 edition promising "a LIKENESS of the AUTHOR."[13] The *Notes on Virginia* became a major vehicle for the circulation of the image of Jefferson drawn by Edward Savage. In addition, at least two other publications that had the potential for mass distribution contain engravings taken from the Savage print.

Jefferson's inauguration on March 4, 1801, was a momentous event, marking the first transfer of political power in the national government from one political party to another. His address on that

[11] Thomas Jefferson, *Notes on the State of Virginia* (8th American ed., Boston: David Carlisle, for Thomas & Andrews, J. West, West & Greenleaf, J. White & Co., E. & S. Larkin, J. Nancrede, Manning & Loring, Boston; Thomas & Thomas, Walpole, N.H.; and B. B. Macanulty, Salem, 1801).

[12] The Virginia Historical Society has copies of the Boston 1801 edition in both the signed and unsigned states. The lettering on the signed plate is very faint.

[13] *American Citizen* (New York), April 4, 1801.

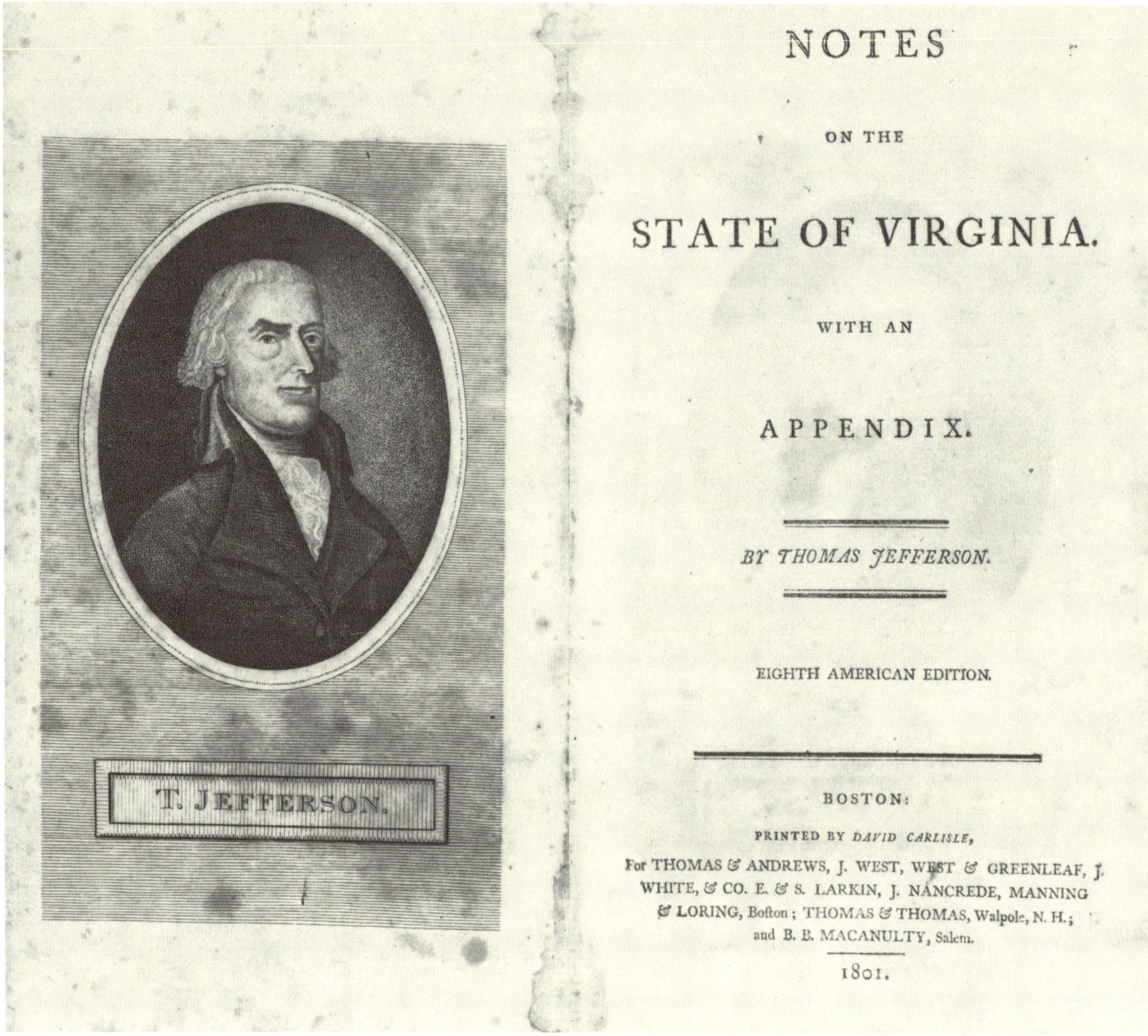

Fig. 5. Jefferson's Notes on the State of Virginia, *Boston, 1801. Frontispiece and title page. Engraving by Enoch G. Gridley*

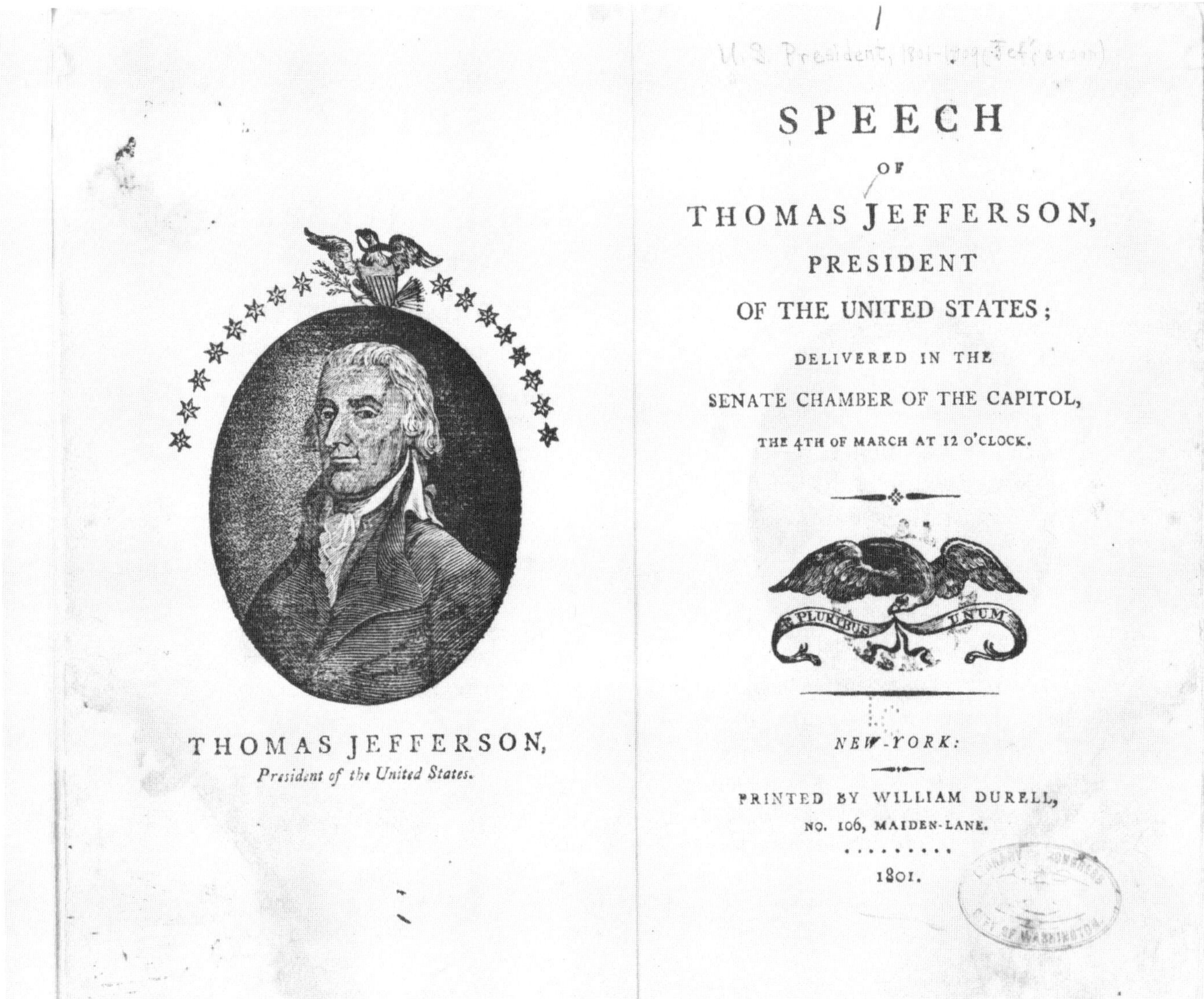

THOMAS JEFFERSON,
President of the United States.

SPEECH
OF
THOMAS JEFFERSON,
PRESIDENT
OF THE UNITED STATES;
DELIVERED IN THE
SENATE CHAMBER OF THE CAPITOL,
THE 4TH OF MARCH AT 12 O'CLOCK.

PLURIBUS UNUM

NEW-YORK:
PRINTED BY WILLIAM DURELL,
NO. 106, MAIDEN-LANE.
1801.

Fig. 6. Jefferson's first inaugural address, printed by William Durell, New York, 1801. Frontispiece and title page. Engraving by unknown artist occasion was a document of wide popular interest. Samuel Harrison Smith, editor of the Washington *National Intelligencer*, having received an advance copy of the speech from Jefferson, offered printed copies for sale immediately after the inaugural ceremony,[14] and the address was soon being published in newspapers throughout the country. It was also widely reprinted in broadsides and pamphlets. Among the various publications, two pamphlet editions have been found containing prints of Jefferson as frontispieces, and one broadside has been discovered with a miniature likeness of the president at the top.[15] The most elaborate edition of Jefferson's inaugural address was published in New York by William Durell.[16] The frontispiece wood engraving offers Jefferson's portrait embellished with a border containing sixteen stars (one for each state in the Union) and dominated by an eagle at the top (fig. 6). The portrait was derived from Edward Savage, though neither Savage nor the engraver was identified.

In addition to the engravings after Savage that appeared in the publications described above, Savage's mezzotint suitable for framing continued to be sold. After Savage moved from Philadelphia to New York in 1801, he ran advertisements in the Philadelphia *Aurora* reminding Philadelphians that his prints of Jefferson (and others) could be purchased at S. Kennedy's, 129 Chesnut Street, in Philadelphia.[17] Presumably he was also selling the prints in New

[14]See Noble E. Cunningham, Jr., *The Process of Government under Jefferson* (Princeton, N.J., 1978), pp. 8–9.

[15]See pp. 33–37 below.

[16]*Speech of Thomas Jefferson, President of the United States; Delivered in the Senate Chamber of the Capitol, the 4th of March at 12 o'clock* (New York: Printed by William Durell, 1801). Rare Book Division, Lib. Cong.

[17]*Aurora*, June 2, July 4, 1801. The advertisement is dated May 23.

York. Study of the images of President Jefferson before the public during his presidency thus reveals that the likeness drawn by Edward Savage, so little appreciated today, was a major source from which many of Jefferson's contemporaries drew their impressions of the physical appearance of the president.

Fig. 7. Thomas Jefferson. Engraving by David Edwin, 1800

CHAPTER III

Variations on a Portrait by Rembrandt Peale

NO PORTRAIT WAS MORE IMPORTANT IN ESTABLISHING the contemporary public image of Jefferson as president than the first life portrait painted by Rembrandt Peale in 1800. That arresting portrait (Appendix, plate IV), which captured Jefferson at age fifty-seven on the eve of his election to the presidency, was long lost from public view; but it was identified in 1959 and now hangs in the White House. It was from engravings, however, rather than the original painting that the public came to know Peale's portrait. Although no engraving gave justice to the penetrating likeness, no other portrait was as influential during Jefferson's lifetime in supplying the image that engravers, with varying degrees of skill, copied in both America and Europe.

The first engraving of Peale's portrait was made by David Edwin (fig. 7), an English-born engraver who had come to Philadelphia in 1797 and by 1800 was beginning to emerge as an engraver of merit.[1] William Dunlap judged Edwin as "the first good en-

[1]David McNeely Stauffer, *American Engravers upon Copper and Steel*, 2 vols. (New York, 1907), 1: 76–77; Charles R. Hildeburn, "A Contribution to a Catalogue of the Engraved Works of David Edwin," *Pennsylvania Magazine of History and Biography* 18 (1894): 97–118; Mantle Fielding, "The Engraved Works of David Edwin," ibid., 28 (1904): 420–27; Mantle Fielding, "David Edwin, Engraver," ibid., 29 (1905): 79–88, 320–25.

graver of the human countenance, that appeared in this country,"[2] but Edwin's likeness of Jefferson is less than faithful to the original portrait, with a noticeable flatness of head not found in the original. Rembrandt Peale was strongly dissatisfied with Edwin's engraving. In a letter in 1801 accepting a request from President-elect Jefferson to paint a replica of his portrait, Peale declared that he "was much mortified at the abominable abuse of this Picture in the Print first made from it" — an allusion that could only refer to Edwin's print.[3] That engraving is signed by Edwin, and Peale is identified as the painter of the portrait. Inscribed "Published by J. Savage 1800," the first prints carry the inscription "Thomas Jefferson Esqr. Vice President of the United States." After Jefferson's election as president, "Vice" was erased from the plate.[4] Edwin's prints were being offered for sale as early as the summer of 1800,[5]

[2]Dunlap, *History . . . of the Arts of Design*, 2: 199. See also Harold E. Dickson, *Arts of the Young Republic: The Age of William Dunlap* (Chapel Hill, N.C., 1968), p. 62.

[3]Rembrandt Peale to Jefferson, Mar. 1, 1801, Tucker-Coleman Collection, College of William and Mary. Jefferson asked for the copy, "intended for a friend who has expressed a wish for it," in a letter to Charles Willson Peale, Feb. 21, 1801, soon after his election as president by the House of Representatives, Feb. 17, 1801 (photostatic copy, Peale Papers, American Philosophical Society). Rembrandt Peale reported the completion of the replica in a letter to Jefferson, Mar. 24, 1801, Letters of Application and Recommendation for Office during the Administration of Thomas Jefferson, RG 59, National Archives.

[4]Both states are listed in Stanislaus V. Henkels, comp., *The Unique [Hampton L. Carson] Collection of Engraved Portraits of Thomas Jefferson, Benjamin Franklin, and Gilbert Mottier de La Fayette* (Philadelphia, [1904]), nos. 1086, 1087. Henkels reproduced the first state.

[5]On Mar. 7, 1801, William Pardoe, whom Mathew Carey had sought to enlist to sell his 1801 engraving of Jefferson (see below, p. 48) wrote to Carey from Boston that "the print of Mr. Jefferson engraved by Edwin was sold in Boston last summer by Mr. Savage"

Fig. 8. Thomas Jefferson. Engraving by Enoch G. Gridley, Boston, 1801

Fig. 9. Thomas Jefferson. Engraving by John Norman, ca. 1801

and his engraving was soon being pirated by other engravers. Enoch G. Gridley copied it in a print signed "E G Gridley Sc. State St. Boston" (fig. 8) that closely resembles Edwin's engraving. Far superior in execution to the copy that Gridley made of the Savage image for the Boston 1801 edition of Jefferson's *Notes on the State of Virginia*, this print almost certainly was the one that Gridley advertised in a notice in the Boston *Independent Chronicle*, July 2, 1801, offering "a few of the first impressions from a new engraving of THOMAS JEFFERSON, Esq., *President of the United States*, to be sold by E. G. Gridley. Inquire at No. 10, State-Street."[6] A similar close copy of Edwin's 1800 engraving was made by another Boston engraver, John Norman, who engraved Edwin's image of Jefferson within a large oval frame (fig. 9).

Edwin's engraving of Rembrandt Peale's portrait was copied not only in Boston but also elsewhere. It was the source of Cornelius Tiebout's engraving of Jefferson published by David Kennedy, 228 Market Street, Philadelphia (fig. 10). Under an oval-framed portrait a two-line inscription identifies "Thomas Jefferson, Vice President of the U.S." The engraving is signed by Tiebout, but the artistic source of the portrait was not identified until a later and

(Mathew Carey Correspondence, Lea and Febiger Collection, Historical Society of Pennsylvania).

[6] The notice also ran in the issues of July 27 extra and Aug. 6, 1801.

Fig. 10. Thomas Jefferson. Engraving by Cornelius Tiebout, Philadelphia, 1800

Fig. 11. Thomas Jefferson. Engraving by Cornelius Tiebout, Philadelphia, ca. 1801–4

THE

LITERARY MAGAZINE,

AND

AMERICAN REGISTER.

No. 12. SEPTEMBER, 1804. Vol. II.

FOR THE LITERARY MAGAZINE.

THOMAS JEFFERSON.

WITH A PORTRAIT.

THE biography of such a man as Thomas Jefferson can only be drawn up by his own hand, and a true judgment of his merits can only be formed by future generations. When the animosities of the present age have been laid asleep by time, his character and actions may rise to the view in their native and proper colours, and the meed of blame or of praise will be conferred on him, in the degree to which he is justly entitled to it.

In consequence of living in a country, where civil liberty is enjoyed with fewer curbs and restraints than were ever before known; where the honours and riches of the state are open to unbounded competition; where the voluntary suffrages of mankind are the only passport to political power, and their suffrages are influenced by the esteem which individuals may be able to acquire for their wisdom and virtue, the intellectual and moral character of the candidates for public favour become objects of universal and rigid scrutiny: and such is the influence of the passions, that the same man, and the same conduct, is the worst or best, the brightest or darkest, according to the medium through which the gazer examines it. As our passions and interests dictate, our competitors are transformed into monsters and demons, and our partizans or champions into angels and divinities: every faulty speck in the character of the former spreads a deep and horrid black over the whole surface, while the dark spots in the *disk* of the latter are wholly overpowered and lost in the blaze of surrounding brightness.

All this has been eminently true of our present subject. No man has been more applauded or more censured, because no man's situation has been connected in a more intimate manner with the hopes and fears of his fellow citizens. A large number have laboured for his elevation, with all the zeal which our own interest is sure to inspire; wh. : a number, scarcely less considerable, have laboured to degrade him, with all the perseverance and anxiety which men usually display to prevent their own fall.

In this state of things, it would be highly absurd, in a publication like

VOL. II. NO. XII. 1

Fig. 12. The Literary Magazine, and American Register, *Philadelphia, September 1804. Engraving by Cornelius Tiebout, 1800*

larger copy of the portrait published by Augustus Day, 38 Chesnut Street, Philadelphia, bore the identification "R. Peale Pinxt." — "C. Tiebout Scuplt." (fig. 11). Day's publication carries only the title "Thomas Jefferson," suggesting that it appeared after Jefferson's elevation from the vice-presidency.[7]

Jefferson's election to the presidency did not, however, make all of the prints struck from Tiebout's vice-presidential plate unusable. In July 1804 the editor of *The Literary Magazine, and American Register* announced plans to publish a series of "the portraits of all eminent and illustrious men among his countrymen" with "no regard to party animosities and divisions."[8] The series began with the portraits of the presidents — Washington appearing in the July

[7]Day was at 38 Chesnut Street in Philadelphia in 1801 (*Aurora*, July 4, 1801) and is listed at this address in Philadelphia directories until 1805, thus dating the print in the period 1801 to 1805.

[8]*The Literary Magazine, and American Register* (Philadelphia), 2 (July 1804): 243.

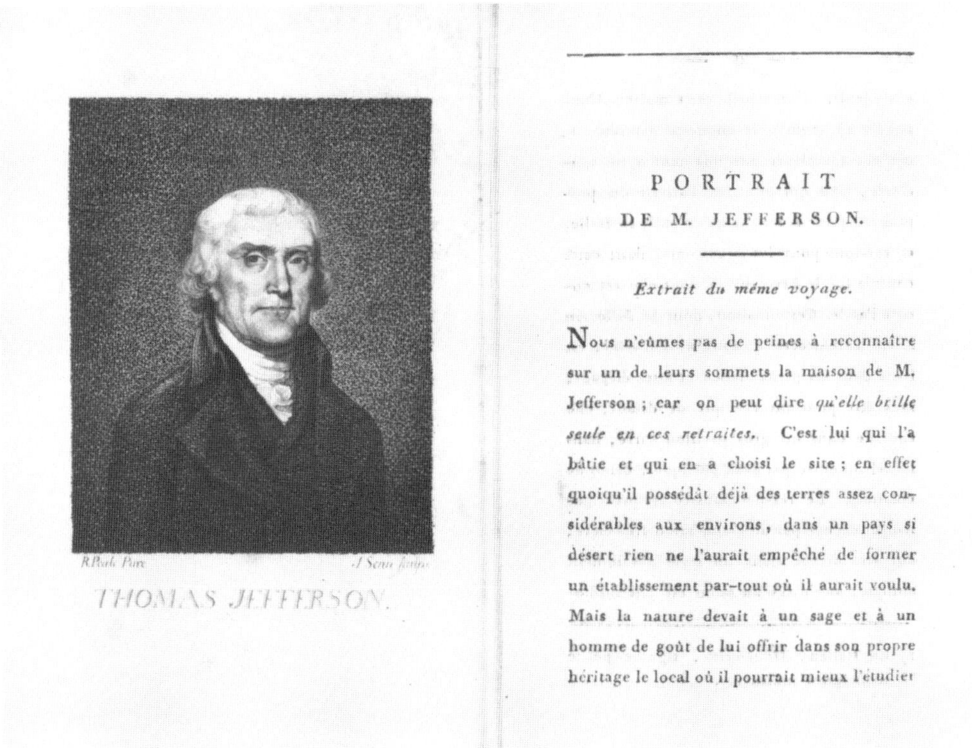

PORTRAIT
DE M. JEFFERSON.

Extrait du même voyage.

Nous n'eûmes pas de peines à reconnaître sur un de leurs sommets la maison de M. Jefferson ; car on peut dire *qu'elle brille seule en ces retraites.* C'est lui qui l'a bâtie et qui en a choisi le site ; en effet quoiqu'il possédât déjà des terres assez considérables aux environs, dans un pays si désert rien ne l'aurait empêché de former un établissement par-tout où il aurait voulu. Mais la nature devait à un sage et à un homme de goût de lui offrir dans son propre héritage le local où il pourrait mieux l'étudier

Fig. 13. Almanac Americain pour l'Annee 1802. *Engraving by Johannes Senn*

issue and John Adams in August. The portrait of Jefferson that followed in the September 1804 issue was the Tiebout engraving published by David Kennedy in 1800, altered by the cutting off of the second line of the inscription denoting "Vice President of the U.S." (fig. 12). That this was the same print can be seen in the comma remaining after Jefferson's name, and in some copies of the magazine traces also remain of the tops of the letters of the second line that was cut off.[9] Thus, this inadequate likeness, which had been quickly followed by a far superior likeness engraved by Tiebout himself, continued to have extensive distribution at least four years after its initial publication.

Edwin's 1800 engraving, rather than one of its derivatives, was the source of the engraving of Jefferson by Johannes Senn, a Swiss painter and engraver whose work appeared in the *Almanac Americain pour l'Annee 1802* (fig. 13). Published in Philadelphia, the pocket-size, 224-page volume contains four colored plates of "Cos-

[9] Copy at Virginia State Library. The University of Virginia Library has a separate print with the second line similarly cut off.

Fig. 14. Goddess of liberty holding portrait of Jefferson, Salem, Massachusetts, January 15, 1807. Engraving by unknown artist

tume Parisien" and portraits of George Washington and Thomas Jefferson accompanied by extracts from the travel account of the chevalier de Chastellux.[10]

One of the derivatives from Edwin's 1800 engraving, perhaps by Enoch Gridley or John Norman, was the likely source for the portrait of Jefferson that appeared in a rare allegorical print published in Salem, Massachusetts, January 15, 1807 (fig. 14). The fifteen-by-seventeen-inch print, which sold for two dollars, includes a detailed explanation of the drawing, described as follows: "In the Center is the Goddess of Liberty sitting on the Globe supporting on her knee with one Hand the Portrait of THOMAS JEFFERSON, President of the United States. With the other she is pointing him out as the Favorite of the People." In the background a monument displays the portrait of Washington, and more distantly there is a ship. The "rays of glory" from the sixteen stars over the head of the goddess "strike their splendid beam on each Portrait" and also on the vessel at a distance "to denote the protection of Commerce."[11] Though the date and place of publication are inscribed on the plate, it is unsigned, and the engraver has not been identified. The print shows that as late as 1807 the 1800 engraving by Edwin was still a major source for the image of Jefferson that the public saw.

Edwin's 1800 engraving was also the source of a series of engravings published in Europe and America that previously have been attributed to Gilbert Stuart. In his ordering of Stuart's three life portraits of Jefferson, Fiske Kimball concluded that the first portrait painted by Stuart in May 1800 was known only through engravings. Kimball identified the earliest examples as the print

[10] Jefferson's portrait appeared facing p. 211, *Almanac American pour l'Annee 1802* (Philadelphia, [1801]), Rare Book Division, Lib. Cong.

[11] Two prints of this engraving have been located: one is at the Essex Institute, Salem; the other, in the Mabel Brady Garvan Collection, Yale University Art Gallery.

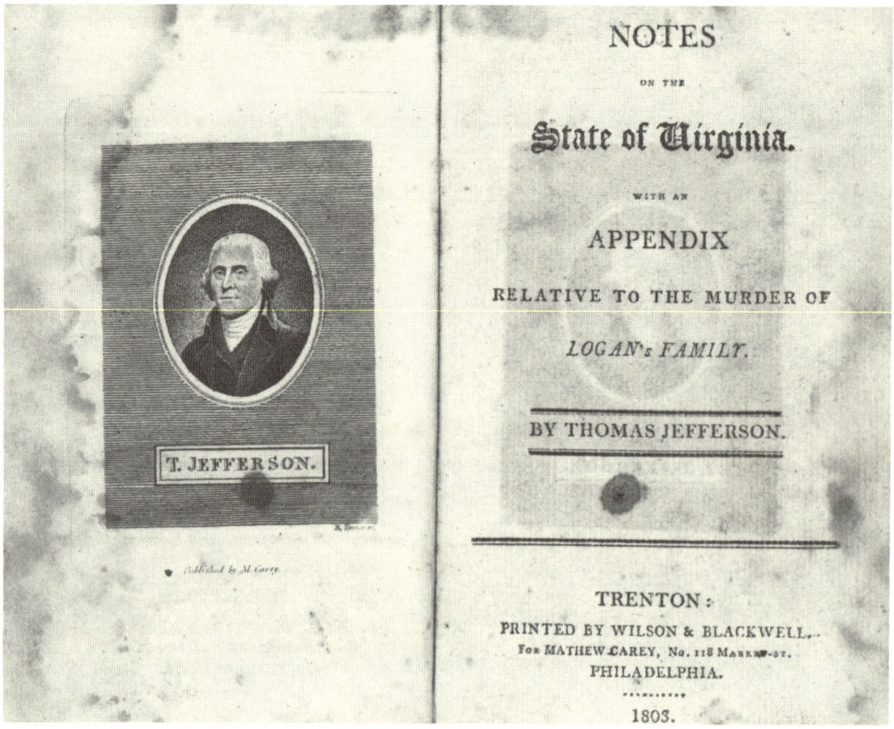

Fig. 15. Jefferson's Notes on the State of Virginia, *Trenton and Philadelphia, 1803. Frontispiece and title page. Engraving by Benjamin Tanner, 1801*

published in London, August 1, 1801, by Edward Orme (see fig. 22) and the engraving copied from it by Friedrich Wilhelm Nettling in Leipzig in 1801 (see fig. 23).[12] Alfred L. Bush accepted Kimball's ordering of Stuart's works as authoritative and offered the engraving issued by Vernor and Hood in London on October 1, 1801 (see fig. 21), as "most probably the most faithful surviving representation of the lost portrait of Jefferson painted in May of 1800 in Philadelphia by Gilbert Stuart." Bush further indicated that the Vernor and Hood print "was copied as the frontispiece to the 1802 Boston edition of Jefferson's *Notes on the State of Virginia*, which in turn was copied the following year for the frontispiece to the Trenton edition of the same work" (see figs. 18 and 15).[13]

A more extensive examination of Jefferson engravings than attempted by either Kimball or Bush, however, shows that the image

[12] Kimball, "Life Portraits of Jefferson," pp. 513–14.

[13] Bush, "Life Portraits of Jefferson," pp. 62, 64.

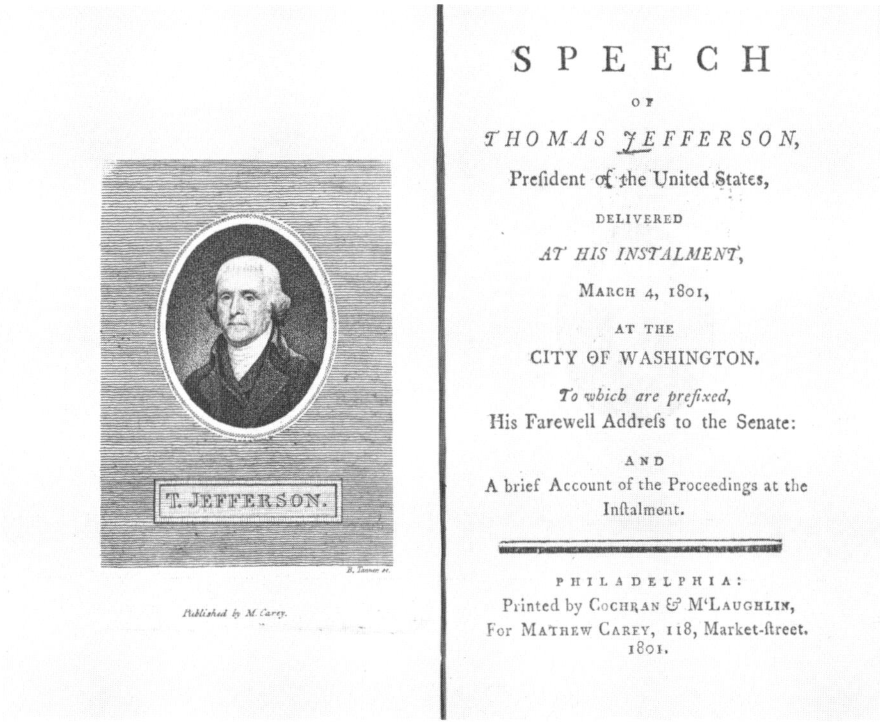

SPEECH
OF
THOMAS JEFFERSON,
Prefident of the United States,
DELIVERED
AT HIS INSTALMENT,
MARCH 4, 1801,
AT THE
CITY OF WASHINGTON.
To which are prefixed,
His Farewell Addrefs to the Senate:
AND
A brief Account of the Proceedings at the Inftalment.

PHILADELPHIA:
Printed by COCHRAN & M'LAUGHLIN,
For MATHEW CAREY, 118, Market-ftreet.
1801.

Fig. 16. Jefferson's first inaugural address, published by Mathew Carey, Philadelphia, 1801. Frontispiece and title page. Engraving by Benjamin Tanner

of Jefferson in the English prints previously had been published in America. The American origins of both the English prints and the print that appeared in the 1802 and the 1803 editions of Jefferson's *Notes on the State of Virginia* can be fully established. The most conclusive evidence is the discovery that the Trenton 1803 edition of Jefferson's work (fig. 15) contains the identical print that had been published by Mathew Carey in March 1801 as the frontispiece to a pamphlet edition of Jefferson's first inaugural address (fig. 16).[14] Carey also used the same engraving in 1801 at the head of a broadside of Jefferson's speech that was printed on both paper

[14]Thomas Jefferson, *Notes on the State of Virginia* (Trenton: Printed by Wilson & Blackwell, for Mathew Carey, Philadelphia, 1803), frontispiece; *Speech of Thomas Jefferson, President of the United States, Delivered at His Instalment, March 4, 1801 at the City of Washington . . .* (Philadelphia: Printed by Cochran & McLaughlin for Mathew Carey, 1801), frontispiece, Rare Book Division, New York Public Library.

SPEECH

OF

THOMAS JEFFERSON, PRESIDENT OF THE UNITED STATES,

DELIVERED

AT HIS INSTALMENT,

MARCH 4, 1801,

AT THE CITY OF WASHINGTON.

FRIENDS, AND FELLOW-CITIZENS,

CALLED upon to undertake the duties of the first executive office of our country, I avail myself of the presence of that portion of my fellow-citizens, which is here assembled, to express my grateful thanks, for the favour with which they have been pleased to look towards me; to declare a sincere consciousness, that the task is above my talents, and that I approach it with those anxious and awful presentiments, which the greatness of the charge, and the weakness of my powers, so justly inspire. A rising nation, spread over a wide and fruitful land....traversing all the seas with the rich productions of their industry....engaged in commerce with nations who feel power and forget right....advancing rapidly to destinies beyond the reach of mortal eye....when I contemplate these transcendent objects, and see the honour, the happiness, and the hopes of this beloved country, committed to [illegible] issue and the auspices of this day, I shrink from the contemplation, and humble myself before the magnitude of the undertaking. Utterly, indeed, should I despair, did not the presence of many, whom I here see, remind me, that, in the other high authorities, provided by our constitution, I shall find resources of wisdom, of virtue, and of zeal, on which to rely under all difficulties. To you, then, gentlemen, who are charged with the sovereign functions of legislation, and to those associated with you, I look with encouragement for that guidance and support, which may enable us to steer, with safety, the vessel in which we are all embarked, amidst the conflicting elements of a troubled world.

During the contest of opinion, through which we have past, the animation of discussions and of exertions, has sometimes worn an aspect which might impose on strangers, unused to think freely, and to speak and to write what they think: but this being now decided by the voice of the nation, announced according to the rules of the constitution, all will, of course, arrange themselves under the will of the law, and unite in common efforts, for the common good. All, too, will bear in mind this sacred principle....that though the will of the majority is, in all cases, to prevail, that will, to be rightful, must be reasonable....that the minority possess their equal rights, which equal laws must protect, and to violate would be oppression. Let us then, fellow-citizens, unite with one heart, and one mind. Let us restore to social intercourse, that harmony and affection, without which, liberty, and even life itself, are but dreary things. And let us reflect, that, having banished from our land, that religious intolerance, under which mankind so long bled and suffered, we have yet gained little, if we countenance a political intolerance, as despotic, as wicked, and capable of as bitter and bloody persecutions.

During the throes and convulsions of the ancient world....during the agonizing spasms of infuriated man, seeking, through blood and slaughter, his long-lost liberty ....it was not wonderful that the agitation of the billows should reach even this distant and peaceful shore,...that this should be more felt and feared by some, and less by others....and should divide opinions, as to measures of safety. But every difference of opinion is not a difference of principle. We have called by different names, brethren of the same principle. WE ARE ALL REPUBLICANS; WE ARE ALL FEDERALISTS. If there be any among us, who would wish to dissolve this union, or to change its republican form, let them stand undisturbed, as monuments of the safety with which error of opinion may be tolerated, where reason is left free to combat it. I know, indeed, that some honest men fear that a republican government cannot be strong....that this government is not strong enough. But would the honest patriot, in the full tide of successful experiment, abandon a government which has so far kept us free and firm, on the theoretic and visionary fear, that this government, the world's best hope, may, by possibility, want energy to preserve itself?....I trust not....I believe this, on the contrary, the strongest government on earth....I believe it the only one, where every man, at the call of the law, would fly to the standard of the law, and would meet invasions of the public order as his own personal concern. Sometimes it is said, that man cannot be trusted with the government of himself. Can he then be trusted with the government of others? Or have we found angels, in the form of kings, to govern him? Let history answer this question.

Let us, then, with courage and confidence, pursue our own federal and republican principles....our attachment to union and representative government. Kindly separated, by nature and a wide ocean, from the exterminating havoc of one quarter of the globe....too high-minded to endure the degradations of the others....possessing a chosen country, with room enough for our descendents to the thousandth and thousandth generation....entertaining a due sense of our equal right to the use of our own faculties....to the acquisitions of our own industry....to honour and confidence from our fellow-citizens; resulting not from birth, but from our actions, and their sense of them....enlightened by a benign religion, professed, indeed, and practised in various forms, yet all of them inculcating honesty, truth, temperance, gratitude, and the love of man....acknowledging and adoring an over-ruling Providence, which, by all its dispensations, proves that it delights in the happiness of man here, and his greater happiness hereafter....with all these blessings, what more is necessary to make us a happy and a prosperous people?....Still one thing more, fellow-citizens, a wise and frugal government, which shall restrain men from injuring one another; shall leave them otherwise free to regulate their own pursuits of industry and improvement; and shall not take from the mouth of labor the bread it has earned. This is the sum of good government; and this is necessary to close the circle of our felicities.

About to enter, fellow-citizens, on the exercise of duties, which comprehend every thing dear and valuable to you, it is proper you should understand what I deem the essential principles of our government, and consequently those which ought to shape its administration. I will compress them within the narrowest compass they will bear, stating the general principle, but not all its limitations. Equal and exact justice to all men, of whatever state or persuasion, religious or political....peace, commerce, and honest friendship with all nations....entangling alliances with none....the support of the state governments in all their rights, as the most competent administrations for our domestic concerns, and the surest bulwarks against anti-republican tendencies....the preservation of the general government in its whole constitutional vigor, as the sheet anchor of our peace at home, and safety abroad....a jealous care of the right of election by the people....a mild and safe corrective of abuses, which are lopped by the sword of revolution, where peaceable remedies are unprovided....absolute acquiescence in the decisions of the majority, the vital principle of republics, from which is no appeal but to force, the vital principle and immediate parent of despotism....a well-disciplined militia, our best reliance in peace, and for the first moments of war, till regulars may relieve them....the supremacy of the civil over the military authority....economy in the public expence, that labor may be lightly burdened....the honest payment of our debts, and sacred preservation of public faith....encouragement of agriculture, and of commerce, as its handmaid....the diffusion of information, and arraignment of all abuses at the bar of the public reason....freedom of religion....freedom of the press....and freedom of person, under the protection of the habeas corpus, and trial by juries impartially selected. These principles form the bright constellation, which has gone before us, and guided our steps through an age of revolution and reformation. The wisdom of our sages, and blood of our heroes, have been devoted to their attainment. They should be the creed of our political faith....the text of civic instruction....the touchstone by which to try the services of those we trust: and should we wander from them, in moments of error or alarm, let us hasten to retrace our steps, and to regain the road which alone leads to peace, liberty, and safety.

I repair, then, fellow citizens, to the post you have assigned me. With experience enough in subordinate offices, to have seen the difficulties of this, the greatest of all, I have learned to expect, that it will rarely fall to the lot of imperfect man, to retire from this station, with the reputation, and the favor, which bring him into it. Without pretensions to that high confidence you reposed in our first and greatest revolutionary character, whose pre-eminent services had entitled him to the first place in his country's love, and destined for him the fairest page in the volume of faithful history, I ask so much confidence only, as may give firmness and effect to the legal administration of your affairs. I shall often go wrong, through defect of judgment. When right, I shall often be thought wrong, by those whose positions will not command a view of the whole ground. I ask your indulgence for my own errors, which will never be intentional; and your support against the errors of others, who may condemn what they would not, if seen in all its parts. The approbation implied by your suffrage, is a great consolation to me for the past: and my future solicitude will be, to retain the good opinion of those who have bestowed it in advance, to conciliate that of others by doing them all the good in my power, and to be instrumental to the happiness and freedom of all.

Relying, then, on the patronage of your good will, I advance with obedience to the work, ready to retire from it whenever you become sensible how much better choices it is in your power to make. And may that infinite Power, which rules the destinies of the universe, lead our councils to what is best, and give them a favourable issue, for our peace and prosperity.

THOMAS JEFFERSON.

THIRD EDITION.

PHILADELPHIA, PUBLISHED BY MATHEW CAREY.

H. MAXWELL, PRINTER.

and satin (fig. 17).[15] The small engraving was by Benjamin Tanner, and the prints appearing in the pamphlet edition are signed by him. They are also inscribed "Published by M. Carey." Carey's account books show that he paid Tanner ten dollars on June 30, 1800, for "Engraving small Portrait of Jefferson."[16]

Carey's account books also reveal that Tanner's engraving of Jefferson was extensively available to the public in March and April 1801 in both the pamphlet and the broadside editions of his inaugural address. On March 11, 1801, John Means charged Carey three dollars for "printing 300 portraits of Jefferson at the Head of his Speech." During the remainder of March, Means printed another 279 Jefferson portraits on the paper broadsides, 74 satin copies, and 500 prints of the portrait for the frontispiece of the pamphlet edition. During April and May 1801, Means supplied another 550 prints of the Jefferson engraving for pamphlet publication and impressed the portrait on 50 additional paper and 15 satin broadsides.[17] Carey's records for March, April, and May 1801 thus show that he had a total of 1,050 prints struck from Tanner's plate for pamphlet publication, 629 impressions made on paper broadsides, and 89 on satin prints. With the number of the separate prints made, it would not have been surprising for Carey to have had copies left to be used in his 1803 edition of Jefferson's *Notes on the State of Virginia* (see fig. 15).

[15] *Speech of Thomas Thomas Jefferson, President of the United States, Delivered at His Instalment, March 4, 1801, at the City of Washington* (3d ed., Philadelphia, published by Mathew Carey, H. Maxwell, printer, [1801]). The Massachusetts Historical Society has copies of both the paper and the satin broadsides.

[16] Account books, no. 5870, Mathew Carey Papers, American Antiquarian Society.

[17] Account books, nos. 5783, 5757, 5782, 5784, 5751, 5753, 5755, 5761, 5763, 5764, ibid. John Means did only the printing of the engraved plate. The pamphlet was printed by Cochran & McLaughlin and the broadside by Hugh Maxwell. Maxwell printed over 600 copies of the broadside for Carey in Mar. 1801 (Account books, nos. 5747, 5791, ibid.).

Fig. 17. Broadside of Jefferson's first inaugural address, published by Mathew Carey, Philadelphia, 1801. Engraving by Benjamin Tanner

Tanner's small and no doubt hastily done engraving (for he charged Carey only ten dollars for the plate) taken from Edwin's 1800 engraving, or from one of its derivatives, must have been seen by hundreds of Americans. Carey's pamphlet and broadside editions of Jefferson's inaugural address were widely advertised in the newspapers. Within a week after Jefferson's inauguration Carey was advertising that the work was in the press, and on March 14, 1801, he announced the broadside edition as "just published, . . . elegantly printed (by Maxwell, in his best manner) on superfine wove paper, with a miniature likeness at the top." The price of one quarter dollar brought it within the reach of the ordinary person, though the more discriminating purchasers were offered prints on satin "at different prices from one dollar and a quarter, to one dollar and three quarters, according to the quality of the satin."[18] That sales were strong is indicated by the fact that Carey was advertising the third edition of the broadside by March 27, and his accounts with John Means show that in mid-March, Means was making impressions of the portraits almost daily.[19] Carey sent Jefferson a copy of the broadside, presumably the paper edition, for later at the president's request he sent him a copy of the satin print.[20]

Carey's prints were available not only in Philadelphia but also in other leading cities. The *Virginia Argus* in April offered the broadside in Richmond for twenty-five cents and used Carey's description of the speech as "elegantly printed on superfine paper, with a Miniature Likeness at the top." Later the *Virginia Argus* advertised the pamphlet edition. The *Raleigh Register* in May 1801 published a list of "new and interesting Political Pamphlets" that

[18] *Aurora*, Mar. 9, 14, 1801. A similar advertisement dated April 7, 1801, appeared in the *Pennsylvania Gazette* (Philadelphia), April 15, 1801.

[19] *Aurora*, Mar. 27, 1801; Account books, no. 5782, Carey Papers, Am. Antiq. Soc.

[20] Carey to Jefferson, Mar. 17, 31, 1801, Jefferson Papers, Coolidge Collection, Mass. Hist. Soc., microfilm edition, reel 5.

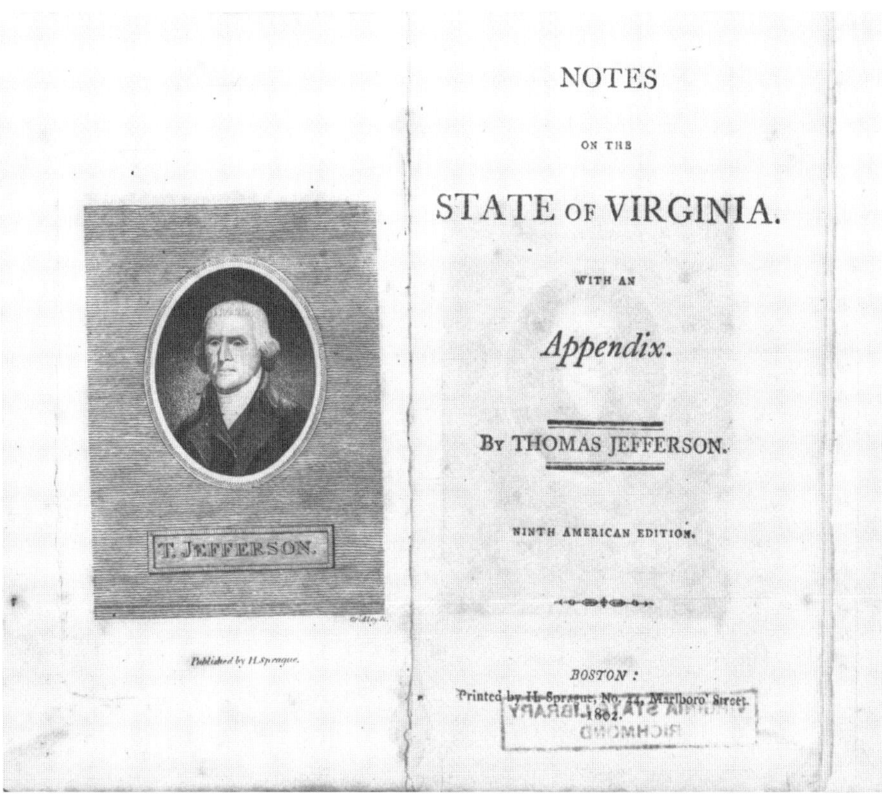

Fig. 18. Jefferson's Notes on the State of Virginia, *Boston, 1802. Frontispiece and title page. Engraving by Enoch G. Gridley*

included "Thomas Jefferson's Speech on his Installation to the Presidency of the U. States, in a Pamphlet, and on a Sheet for framing, each adorned with his Portrait."[21] Thus, Tanner's engraving of Jefferson was widely available in the United States soon after Jefferson's inauguration, and it seems likely that this was the source of Enoch G. Gridley's similar engraving that was published in the Boston 1802 edition of Jefferson's *Notes on the State of Virginia* (fig. 18).[22]

As early as April 1801 Tanner's engraving was also available in the British Isles, for a print derived from it appeared that month in *Walker's Hibernian Magazine: or, Compendium of Entertaining Knowledge* (fig. 19) published in Dublin. Not only can the deriva-

[21] *Virginia Argus* (Richmond), April 10, 28, June 16, 23, 30, 1801; *Raleigh Register*, May 19, 26, June 2, 16, 1801.

[22] Thomas Jefferson, *Notes on the State of Virginia* (9th American ed., Boston: Printed by H. Sprague, 1802), frontispiece.

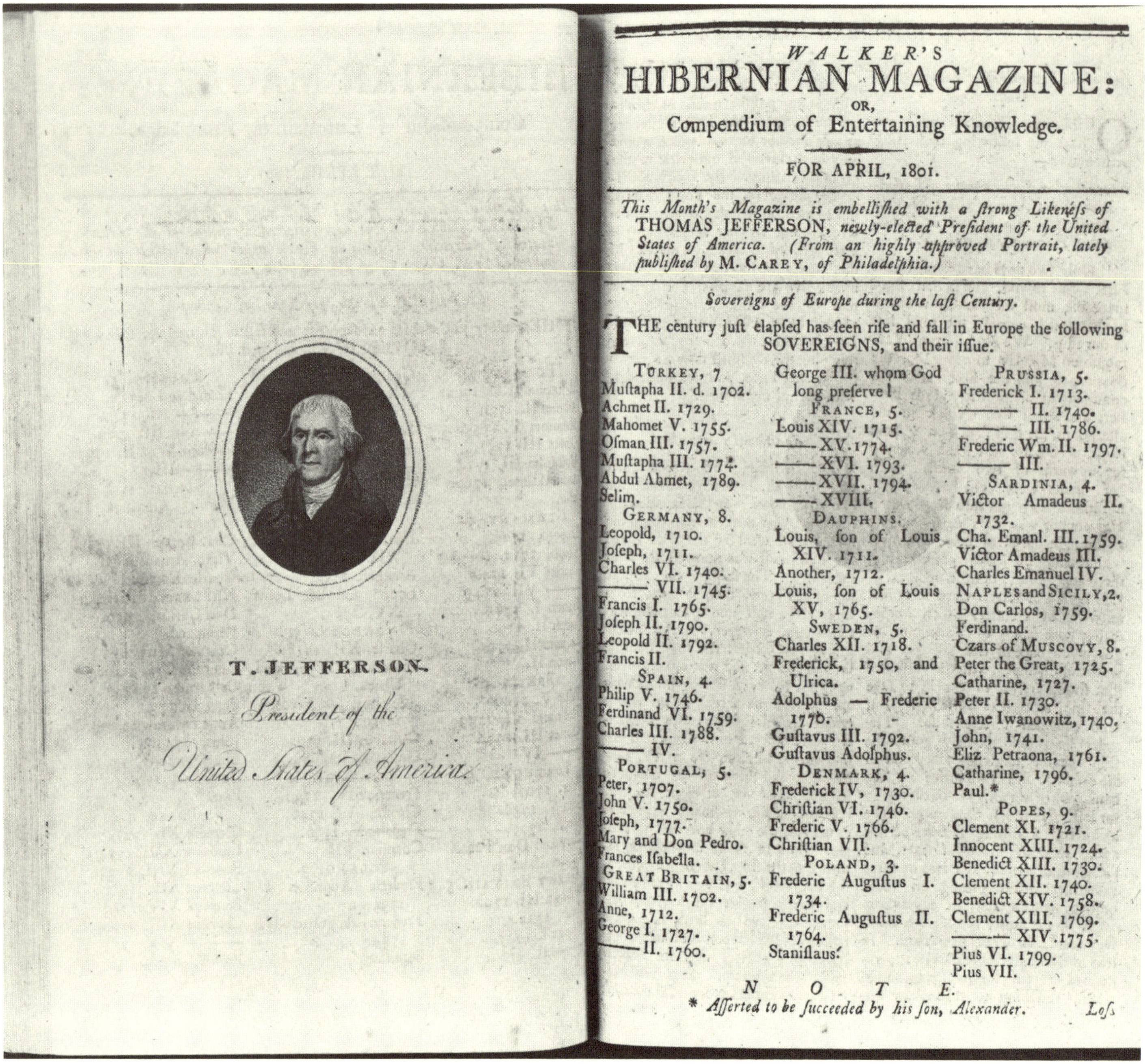
T. JEFFERSON.

President of the United States of America.

WALKER'S

HIBERNIAN MAGAZINE:

OR,

Compendium of Entertaining Knowledge.

FOR APRIL, 1801.

This Month's Magazine is embelliſhed with a ſtrong Likeneſs of THOMAS JEFFERSON, *newly-elected Preſident of the United States of America. (From an highly approved Portrait, lately publiſhed by* M. CAREY, *of Philadelphia.)*

Sovereigns of Europe during the laſt Century.

THE century juſt elapſed has ſeen riſe and fall in Europe the following SOVEREIGNS, and their iſſue.

TURKEY, 7.
Muſtapha II. d. 1702.
Achmet II. 1729.
Mahomet V. 1755.
Oſman III. 1757.
Muſtapha III. 1774.
Abdul Ahmet, 1789.
Selim.

GERMANY, 8.
Leopold, 1710.
Joſeph, 1711.
Charles VI. 1740.
——— VII. 1745.
Francis I. 1765.
Joſeph II. 1790.
Leopold II. 1792.
Francis II.

SPAIN, 4.
Philip V. 1746.
Ferdinand VI. 1759.
Charles III. 1788.
——— IV.

PORTUGAL, 5.
Peter, 1707.
John V. 1750.
Joſeph, 1777.
Mary and Don Pedro.
Frances Iſabella.

GREAT BRITAIN, 5.
William III. 1702.
Anne, 1712.
George I. 1727.
——— II. 1760.
George III. whom God long preſerve!

FRANCE, 5.
Louis XIV. 1715.
——— XV. 1774.
——— XVI. 1793.
——— XVII. 1794.
——— XVIII.

DAUPHINS.
Louis, ſon of Louis XIV. 1711.
Another, 1712.
Louis, ſon of Louis XV, 1765.

SWEDEN, 5.
Charles XII. 1718.
Frederick, 1750, and Ulrica.
Adolphus — Frederic 1770.
Guſtavus III. 1792.
Guſtavus Adolphus.

DENMARK, 4.
Frederick IV, 1730.
Chriſtian VI. 1746.
Frederic V. 1766.
Chriſtian VII.

POLAND, 3.
Frederic Auguſtus I. 1734.
Frederic Auguſtus II. 1764.
Staniſlaus.

PRUSSIA, 5.
Frederick I. 1713.
——— II. 1740.
——— III. 1786.
Frederic Wm. II. 1797.
——— III.

SARDINIA, 4.
Victor Amadeus II. 1732.
Cha. Emanl. III. 1759.
Victor Amadeus III.
Charles Emanuel IV.

NAPLES and SICILY, 2.
Don Carlos, 1759.
Ferdinand.

Czars of MUSCOVY, 8.
Peter the Great, 1725.
Catharine, 1727.
Peter II. 1730.
Anne Iwanowitz, 1740.
John, 1741.
Eliz. Petraona, 1761.
Catharine, 1796.
Paul.*

POPES, 9.
Clement XI. 1721.
Innocent XIII. 1724.
Benedict XIII. 1730.
Clement XII. 1740.
Benedict XIV. 1758.
Clement XIII. 1769.
——— XIV. 1775.
Pius VI. 1799.
Pius VII.

N O T E.

* *Aſſerted to be ſucceeded by his ſon, Alexander.* Loſs

Fig. 19. Walker's Hibernian Magazine, *Dublin, April 1801. Engraving by unknown artist*

Fig. 20. Thomas Jefferson. Engraving by John Kay, Edinburgh, 1801

tion be confirmed by visual comparison, but a record of its origin also was provided by the editor, who announced: "This Month's Magazine is embellished with a strong Likeness of THOMAS JEFFERSON, newly-elected President of the United States of America. (From an highly approved Portrait, lately published by M. Carey, of Philadelphia.)"[23]

The influence of the Tanner engraving or of the *Hibernian Magazine* print can be seen in the engraving made by John Kay in Edinburgh and dated 1801 (fig. 20). Kay, a caricaturist, engraver, and miniature painter, ran a small printshop on Parliament Square in Edinburgh, where he filled the window of his shop with his most recent works.[24] His print of Jefferson is not a very good likeness

[23] *Walker's Hibernian Magazine . . . for the Year 1801* (Dublin: Printed by Richard Gibson), pt. 1, p. 193 and print facing p. 193.

[24] [Hugh Patton, ed.], *A Series of Original Portraits and Caricature Etchings by the late John Kay . . . with Biographical Sketches and Illustrative Anecdotes* (1838; rept. Edinburgh, 1877), 1: 3; print of Jefferson, vol. 2, opposite p. 193. The editor indicated that the portrait of Jefferson was etched from "an original miniature" forwarded to Kay from America (ibid., 2: 193).

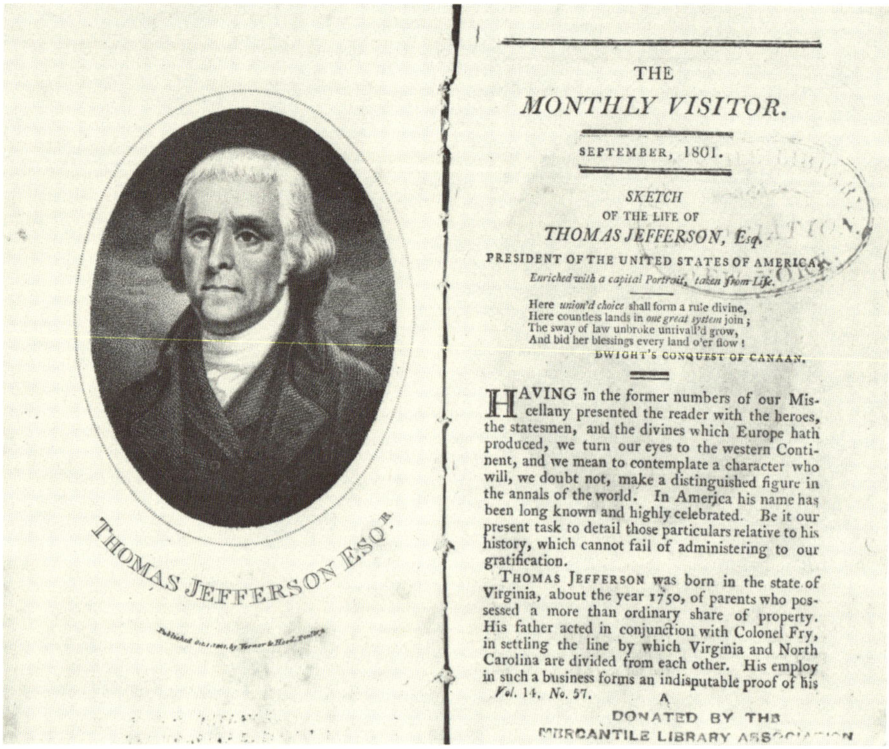
THE
MONTHLY VISITOR.
SEPTEMBER, 1801.
SKETCH
OF THE LIFE OF
THOMAS JEFFERSON, Esq.
PRESIDENT OF THE UNITED STATES OF AMERICA.
Enriched with a capital Portrait, taken from Life.

Here *union'd choice* shall form a rule divine,
Here countless lands in *one great system* join;
The sway of law unbroke unrivall'd grow,
And bid her blessings every land o'er flow!
DWIGHT'S CONQUEST OF CANAAN.

HAVING in the former numbers of our Miscellany presented the reader with the heroes, the statesmen, and the divines which Europe hath produced, we turn our eyes to the western Continent, and we mean to contemplate a character who will, we doubt not, make a distinguished figure in the annals of the world. In America his name has been long known and highly celebrated. Be it our present task to detail those particulars relative to his history, which cannot fail of administering to our gratification.

THOMAS JEFFERSON was born in the state of Virginia, about the year 1750, of parents who possessed a more than ordinary share of property. His father acted in conjunction with Colonel Fry, in settling the line by which Virginia and North Carolina are divided from each other. His employ in such a business forms an indisputable proof of his

Vol. 14. *No.* 57. A

Fig. 21. The Monthly Visitor, *London, September 1801. Engraving published by Vernor and Hood, October 1, 1801*

even of the inadequate Tanner image, but it suggests that the Tanner print was circulating in Britain in 1801.

Carey's print that was copied in Dublin and Edinburgh could also have reached London. In fact, Carey purchased books from Vernor and Hood in London,[25] and he could have sent copies of his print of Tanner's engraving directly to them. But there is no record of this, and it may be supposed that the *Hibernian Magazine* was the most accessible source of the Tanner image. In any event, the Edward Orme print dated August 1, 1801, and the Vernor and Hood engraving dated October 1, 1801, published in *The Monthly Visitor* (London) for September 1801 (fig. 21), could easily have been copied from the plate in the *Hibernian Magazine* or from another derivation of David Edwin's 1800 engraving. The Vernor and Hood engraving, which the editor of *The Monthly Visitor* described as "a capital Portrait, taken from Life," particularly seems

[25] Account books, no. 5999 (Oct. 2, 1800), Carey Papers, Am. Antiq. Soc.

Fig. 22. Thomas Jefferson. Engraving published by Edward Orme, London, August 1, 1801

Fig. 23. Thomas Jefferson. Engraving by Friedrich Wilhelm Nettling, Leipzig, 1801

to follow the Dublin publication. If the print by Edward Orme (fig. 22) is less faithful to the earlier engraving, it may be due in part to the evidence that the engraver superimposed the head of Jefferson on an old plate containing the bust of the composer and musician Muzio Clementi.[26] That either the Orme print or the Vernor and Hood print was engraved from Stuart's first life portrait of Jefferson cannot, in view of the overwhelming evidence to the contrary, be accepted. The inscription "painted by Stuart in America" that appears on the Orme print and was copied by Nettling (fig. 23) must be rejected as unfounded. Despite Bush's assumption to the contrary, the Vernor and Hood print contains no reference to Stuart, and no American engraving of this type has been found attributed to him.

[26] A print with Jefferson's image and Clementi's name was offered for sale in Stanislaus V. Henkels, *The Unequalled Collection of Engraved Portraits of the Presidents of the United States, Belonging to Hon. James T. Mitchell* (Philadelphia, 1907), p. 14. See also Bush, "Life Portraits of Jefferson," p. 63.

The rejection of the engravings that have been attributed to Stuart's painting reopens the question of what that portrait looked like and what happened to it. There is no evidence that the portrait was ever engraved, although Stuart himself advertised in June 1800 that an engraving of this portrait of Jefferson was "preparing under his immediate direction."[27] Since neither the engravings of Washington nor of John Adams announced at the same time ever appeared,[28] it is reasonable to assume that Stuart never carried through with his proposal. Stuart, who told Jefferson he was dissatisfied with his first portrait when he persuaded the president to sit again in 1805, may have rubbed out his first effort after painting the second, as Kimball concluded.[29] The canvas almost certainly was not sent to England for engraving and lost, as some authorities have suggested.[30] In any case, the public never became acquainted with Stuart's first portrait — a painting that Jefferson himself said he liked better than Stuart's second portrait.[31] It was not until the engraving by Robert Field of Stuart's second portrait of Jefferson appeared in 1807 that Stuart's image of the president came before the public.

Before then, many Europeans and Americans as well would see copies of the English prints attributed to Stuart. The Orme print

[27]*Aurora* (Philadelphia), June 12, 1800; *Independent Chronicle* (Boston), June 23, 1800.

[28]William T. Whitley, *Gilbert Stuart* (Cambridge, Mass., 1932), p. 104.

[29]Kimball, "Life Portraits of Jefferson," p. 514.

[30]Bush, "Life Portraits of Jefferson," p. 63; Marvin S. Sadik, *Colonial and Federal Portraits at Bowdoin College* (Brunswick, Me., 1966), p. 158. The present study supports the rejection by both Bush and Sadik of the claim advanced by Orland and Courtney Campbell in *The Lost Portraits of Thomas Jefferson* (Amherst, Mass., 1959) to have discovered Stuart's first painting under a second.

[31]Jefferson to Henry Dearborn, Mar. 26, 1820, Jefferson Papers, Lib. Cong.

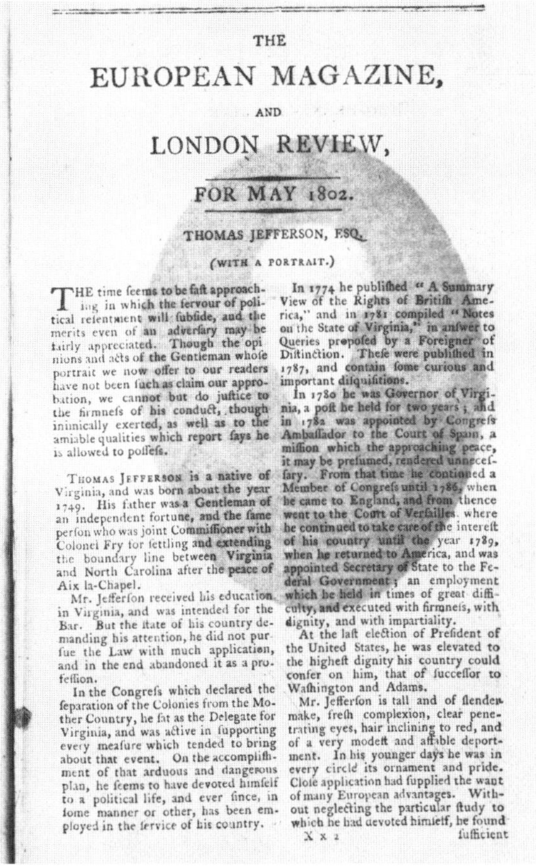

THE

EUROPEAN MAGAZINE,

AND

LONDON REVIEW,

FOR MAY 1802.

THOMAS JEFFERSON, ESQ.

(WITH A PORTRAIT.)

THE time seems to be fast approaching in which the fervour of political resentment will subside, and the merits even of an adversary may be fairly appreciated. Though the opinions and acts of the Gentleman whose portrait we now offer to our readers have not been such as claim our approbation, we cannot but do justice to the firmness of his conduct, though inimically exerted, as well as to the amiable qualities which report says he is allowed to possess.

THOMAS JEFFERSON is a native of Virginia, and was born about the year 1749. His father was a Gentleman of an independent fortune, and the same person who was joint Commissioner with Colonel Fry for settling and extending the boundary line between Virginia and North Carolina after the peace of Aix la-Chapel.

Mr. Jefferson received his education in Virginia, and was intended for the Bar. But the state of his country demanding his attention, he did not pursue the Law with much application, and in the end abandoned it as a profession.

In the Congress which declared the separation of the Colonies from the Mother Country, he sat as the Delegate for Virginia, and was active in supporting every measure which tended to bring about that event. On the accomplishment of that arduous and dangerous plan, he seems to have devoted himself to a political life, and ever since, in some manner or other, has been employed in the service of his country.

In 1774 he published "A Summary View of the Rights of British America," and in 1781 compiled "Notes on the State of Virginia," in answer to Queries proposed by a Foreigner of Distinction. These were published in 1787, and contain some curious and important disquisitions.

In 1780 he was Governor of Virginia, a post he held for two years; and in 1782 was appointed by Congress Ambassador to the Court of Spain, a mission which the approaching peace, it may be presumed, rendered unnecessary. From that time he continued a Member of Congress until 1786, when he came to England, and from thence went to the Court of Versailles, where he continued to take care of the interest of his country until the year 1789, when he returned to America, and was appointed Secretary of State to the Federal Government; an employment which he held in times of great difficulty, and executed with firmness, with dignity, and with impartiality.

At the last election of President of the United States, he was elevated to the highest dignity his country could confer on him, that of successor to Washington and Adams.

Mr. Jefferson is tall and of slender make, fresh complexion, clear penetrating eyes, hair inclining to red, and of a very modest and affable deportment. In his younger days he was in every circle its ornament and pride. Close application had supplied the want of many European advantages. Without neglecting the particular study to which he had devoted himself, he found

X x 2 sufficient

Fig. 24. The European Magazine, and London Review, *May 1802. Engraving published by J. Sewell, June 1, 1802*

was widely available in both Europe and America. It was published in *The European Magazine, and London Review* for May 1802 (fig. 24), with the only alterations in the Orme plate being the addition of the heading "European Magazine" and a change in the publisher. The plate was now identified as "Published by J. Sewell, Cornhill, June 1, 1802." The *European Magazine* also circulated in the United States; it was advertised in American newspapers and regularly read by many Americans, among them St. George Tucker, who had forty-three volumes of the publication in his personal library in Williamsburg.[32] Thus, many Americans saw a print of Jefferson that is inscribed "Painted by Stuart in America," and they

[32] *European Magazine, and London Review* 41(1802): 338 (punctuation added); *Virginia Argus* (Richmond), Sept. 22, 29, Oct. 6, 1801; Richard Beale Davis, *Intellectual Life in Jefferson's Virginia, 1790–1830* (Chapel Hill, N.C., 1964), pp. 76–77, 94–95.

Peale Pinx.

C. Tiebout sculp.

THOMAS JEFFERSON,

President of the United States.

We hold these truths to be self evident,—that all men are created equal; that they are endowed by their Creator with certain unalienable rights; that among these are life, liberty, and the pursuit of happiness. That, to secure these rights, governments are instituted among men, deriving their just powers from the consent of the governed: that whenever any form of government becomes destructive of these ends, it is the right of the people to alter or to abolish it, and to institute new government, laying its foundation on such principles, and organizing its powers in such form, as to them shall seem most likely to effect their safety and happiness.

Declaration of Independence.

Philadelphia Published by M. Carey No. 118 Market St. Feb. 20th 1801 would have had no reason to suspect that this was not the case, though they may have had reason to question the skill of the engraver.

If Rembrandt Peale felt dissatisfied with David Edwin's engraving taken directly from his painting, he must have been outraged by many of the engravings that derived from Edwin's print. Before all of these mutations reached the public, however, Peale was cooperating with Mathew Carey in late 1800 and early 1801 in the engraving of a new plate from his portrait. In his letter of March 1, 1801, in which he confessed to Jefferson his dissatisfaction with Edwin's first engraving of the portrait, Peale wrote that he "was in hopes a Second (just finished) would have been, under my inspection, sufficiently accurate — But the Engraver does not possess the necessary delicacy of hand and eye, and altho' it is much better, am still disappointed. The same cause exists among us for the imperfection of Engraving as of Painting — yet the want of Encouragement cannot repress my fondness for the Art."[33]

This comment by Peale can only refer to the print engraved by Cornelius Tiebout and published by Mathew Carey, February 20, 1801 (fig. 25). Well timed by the enterprising Philadelphia publisher to coincide with Jefferson's inauguration, the engraving is dated three days after Jefferson's election by the House of Representatives. The print was announced as ready for delivery on March 20, just over two weeks after Jefferson's inauguration on March 4.[34] Although disappointing to Peale — even though he found it "much better" than the earlier engraving by Edwin — the engraving, nonetheless, is the best of the engravings to derive from his 1800 life portrait of Jefferson. Tiebout has been judged by one student of American engraving, David McNeely Stauffer, to be "the first American-born professional engraver to produce really

[33] Peale to Jefferson, Mar. 1, 1801, Tucker-Coleman Collection, College of William and Mary.

[34] *Aurora*, Mar. 20, 1801.

Fig. 25. Thomas Jefferson. Engraving by Cornelius Tiebout, published by Mathew Carey, Philadelphia, February 20, 1801

meritorious work";[35] and his stipple engraving of Jefferson on this plate represents one of his best efforts.

The print, which measures slightly under thirteen by nine inches, was well suited for framing. "Thomas Jefferson, President of the United States" is engraved below the portrait, and a two-column excerpt from the Declaration of Independence adds distinctiveness to the print. Publisher Carey, conducting an extensive pre-publication campaign, prepared the following announcement on January 25, 1801:

PROPOSALS
OF
MATHEW CAREY,
For Publishing by Subscription,
AN ELEGANT LIKENESS
(HALF LENGTH)
OF
THOMAS JEFFERSON
President Elect of the U. States
TERMS.

I. The drawing, which is eleven inches by eight and a half, has been executed by Rembrandt Peale, and is allowed by the best judges to be an excellent likeness.

II. It is now engraving, in his best style, by Tiebout, and will be ready for delivery very soon.

III. Price to subscribers, for proof impressions, two dollars — handsomely framed and glazed, five dollars and a half.

IV. Those who procure seven subscribers and engage for the payment, shall have a copy gratis.[36]

Copies of these proposals were mailed throughout the country to agents and friends whom Carey urged to secure subscribers, optimistically predicting a large demand for the prints. To Mason

[35] Stauffer, *American Engravers upon Copper and Steel*, 1: 271–72.

[36] *Virginia Argus*, Mar. 6, 10, 20, 24, 1801, publishing advertisement dated Philadelphia, Jan. 25.

Locke Weems in Virginia, Carey wrote on January 27: "I have engraving a most admirable likeness of Jefferson for two Dollars. By next mail I shall send you proposals, and, in a week, a specimen. By 25 per cent on this you may clear 500 Dollars. For yourself you can readily get 1000 subscribers." Two weeks later he sent Weems a copy of the print and some subscription papers.[37] Parson Weems, perhaps the most active book salesman of his day, covered the Atlantic seaboard from New York to Georgia for Carey. In 1801 and 1802, operating out of his headquarters at Dumfries, Virginia, he traveled to New Jersey and New York and through Delaware and Maryland.[38] "I set out tomorrow — shall take Jefferson," Weems replied to Carey on February 24, and a week later he reported that he had some subscribers for the print. He also advised: "Put some beautiful lines (*poetry*) under Jefferson. They will do great good."[39] Instead, Carey included an excerpt from the Declaration of Independence under Jefferson's portrait.

Offering terms less generous than those to Weems, Carey wrote to Samuel Pleasants, Jr., editor of the Richmond *Virginia Argus*, on February 24: "I enclose a subscription paper for the likeness of Jefferson, of which I also enclose our unfinished proof to show as a specimen. I wish you, at my Expense, to print 40 or 50 or 100 copies of the paper; and to distribute them among your friends in different directions by your post riders. On all the copies you sell I shall allow 20 per cent commission. I trust you will be diligent, and I shall hold myself highly indebted to you." On the same day, he

[37] Carey to Weems, Jan. 27, Feb. 14, 1801, Mathew Carey letter book, Lea and Febiger Collection, Hist. Soc. Pa.

[38] Davis, *Intellectual Life in Jefferson's Virginia*, pp. 79–80; Emily E. F. Skeel, ed., *Mason Locke Weems: His Works and Ways*, 3 vols. (New York, 1929), 2: xxi-xxii.

[39] Weems to Carey, Feb. 24, Mar. 4, 1801, Skeel, ed., *Weems*, 2: 175, 176. Editor Skeel mistakenly considered the first letter as referring to Jefferson's *Notes on the State of Virginia*. Weems repeated the advice regarding poetry (Weems to Carey, Mar. 5, 1801, ibid., 2: 177).

wrote to Congressman Mathew Lyon: "I take the liberty to enclose you some subscription papers for an elegant likeness of the president-elect, of which I send you part of an unfinished proof. Will you be so good to exert yourself to procure now as many subscribers as possible. You shall be entitled to the specified allowance of one for every seven subscribers you procure."[40]

In sending proofs of the print to potential agents for its sale, Carey, whose print would contain the notation "Copy right Secured," was alert to the danger of having the image of Jefferson pirated. He sternly instructed one correspondent: "You will not allow any person whatsoever to have it five minutes out of your possession." Carey was greatly disappointed when William Pardoe of Boston declined to sell the print on the grounds that "the print of Mr. Jefferson engraved by Edwin was sold in Boston last summer by Mr. Savage, should therefore think that very few would now be disposed of." Carey disagreed, writing to Pardoe that he felt "strongly persuaded it would have met with considerable success as to pay amply for your time and trouble." He even offered to pay Pardoe for one week's trial of selling the print, but Pardoe had already returned the engraving.[41]

Although not all of Carey's correspondents agreed to sell the prints, many did. Samuel Pleasants, Jr., published Carey's proposals in the Richmond *Virginia Argus* together with a notice that subscriptions would be received at his printing office "*where a proof specimen of the likeness may be seen*." Pleasants must have had some success; he placed one order for eighteen of the framed prints. Yet, even while filling this order, Carey continued to urge the Richmond editor to be active. "Let me request you to exert yourself to the utmost in the disposal of Jefferson," he wrote to Pleasants on April 9, by which time several competing prints were being advertised

[40] Carey to Pleasants, Feb. 24, 1801, Carey to Lyon, Feb. 24, 1801, Carey letter book, Lea and Febiger Collection, Hist. Soc. Pa.

[41] Carey to William Pardoe, Feb. 25, Mar. 27, 1801, ibid.; Pardoe to Carey, Mar. 7, April 15, 1801, Mathew Carey Correspondence, ibid.

in Philadelphia. "I have a good deal at stake in that print, and may lose considerably by the large number of frames which I bespoke, unless I meet with good encouragement to the southward."[42]

Carey, indeed, had invested heavily in his Jefferson print. He paid Cornelius Tiebout $150 for engraving the plate and an additional $6.64 for the lettering — a substantial fee, clearly designed to obtain a carefully prepared, superior plate.[43] To promote the same end, he also paid Rembrandt Peale $50 "for the use of an Original Portrait of T. Jefferson in making an Engraving."[44] These fees contrast sharply with the $10 that Carey paid Benjamin Tanner for engraving the small plate of Jefferson used on the broadside and pamphlet publications of his inaugural address — which were being sold simultaneously with the larger portrait. For making the impressions from Tiebout's plate, Carey paid John Means $3 per hundred. Between March 7 and June 8, 1801, he secured 800 prints of the Jefferson portrait.[45] More costly than the prints were the frames; most of the difference between the selling price of $2 for the unframed print and $5 for the framed print was accounted for by the actual cost of framing, for which Carey regularly paid $2.75, though he had a few framed for $2.50. At the time Carey

[42] *Virginia Argus*, Mar. 6, 10, 20, 24, 1801; Carey to Pleasants, April 9, 1801, Carey letter book, Lea and Febiger Collection, Hist. Soc. Pa. Although Carey initially announced the price of the framed print at $5.50, he reduced the price to $5.00 when he advertised it for delivery on Mar. 20 (*Aurora*, Mar. 20, 1801). In Richmond, Pleasants, however, continued to charge $5.50 (*Virginia Argus*, May 8, 29, June 9, 12, 30, 1801).

[43] Carey to Cornelius Tiebout, Aug. 19, 21, 1800, account books, nos. 5995, 6892, Carey Papers, Am. Antiq. Soc.

[44] The statement in Carey's account books dated Philadelphia, Dec. 31, 1800, was endorsed by Rembrandt Peale on the same date: "Received in part payment of the above, thirty two Dolls. and forty Cents" (Account books, no. 5807, ibid.).

[45] Carey to John Means, Mar. 7, 27, April 16, June 8, 1801, account books, nos. 5773, 5757, 5759, 5787, ibid.

wrote worriedly to Pleasants about his investment in frames, he had invested over $600 in having 224 of the Jefferson prints framed. David Kennedy, a carver and gilder whose shop at 228 Market Street in Philadelphia was not far from Carey's bookstore at 118 Market Street, had done most of the work, framing 182 Jefferson prints at $2.75 each. Augustus Day had provided frames for 42 Jefferson prints at $2.50 each.[46]

These details on the conduct of Carey's business provide rare information about the number of Jefferson prints that were sold. Despite Carey's apprehensions, sales were good, for in May and June 1801 he had another twenty Jefferson prints framed, and in July he ordered an additional twenty-four.[47] The total number of prints framed from March through July 1801 came to 268 at a cost of $726.50. Carey's success showed that a market existed for framed portraits of the president at five dollars a piece. A discriminating collector could have had Rembrandt Peale paint a replica of his original Jefferson portrait, from which the engraving was made, for thirty dollars, but Jefferson is the only patron known to have done so.[48] Potential buyers for the unframed print at two dollars were more numerous, but as Carey's correspondence indicates, advertising and sales efforts were required. One salesman's record, labeled "An Account of Money received on the sale of Jefferson's Portrait and expenses of the Journey from Friday 27th February to Saturday 28th March 1801," listed the sale of fourteen unframed Jefferson prints in Washington and Georgetown, three in Alexandria, and ten in Baltimore and one framed print in Baltimore. Among the Washington purchasers, from this or another agent, was the Department of State, where on March 19, 1801, someone

[46] Account books, nos. 5680, 5682, 5575, ibid.

[47] Account books, no. 6851, ibid.

[48] Rembrandt Peale to Jefferson, Mar. 1, 1801, Tucker-Coleman Collection, College of William Mary; Peale to Jefferson, Mar. 24, 1801, Letters of Application and Recommendation, RG 59, National Archives.

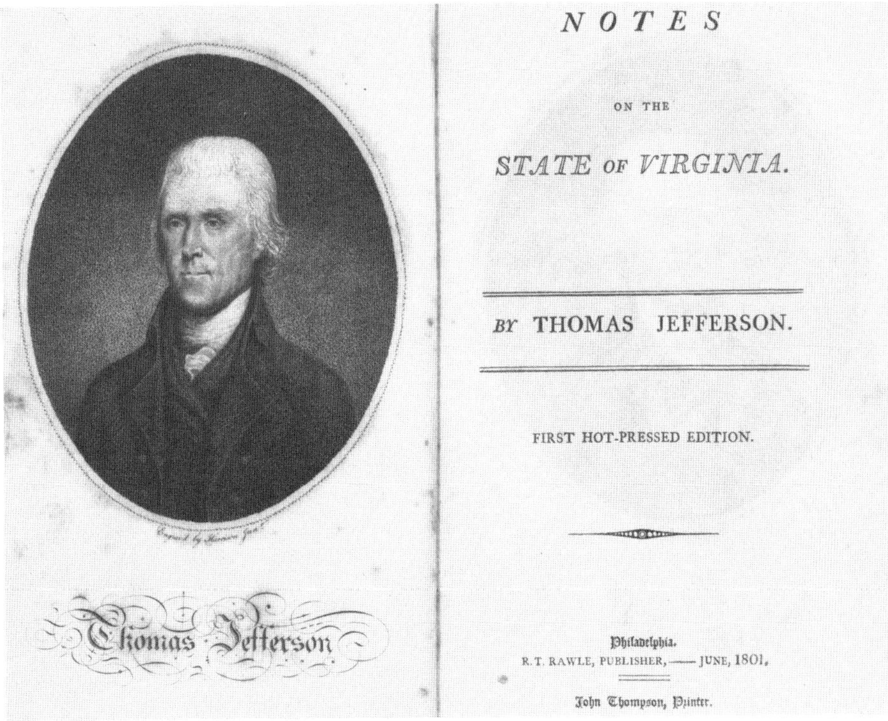

Fig. 26. Jefferson's Notes on the State of Virginia, *Philadelphia, June 1801. Frontispiece and title page. Engraving by William Harrison, Jr.*

recorded in the department's daybook for miscellaneous and contingent expenses an expenditure for "a print of Thomas Jefferson, President of the U States 2.00."[49]

Although Carey's print is inscribed "Copy right Secured," it did not escape being used as a source by other engravers. William Harrison, Jr., must have used it for his engraving of Jefferson that was published as the frontispiece to a major new edition of Jefferson's *Notes on the State of Virginia* that appeared in Philadelphia in June 1801 (fig. 26)[50] Tiebout himself copied his own work commissioned by Carey when he engraved a full-length portrait of Jef-

[49]Account books, no. 5834, Carey Papers, Am. Antiq. Soc.; Daybook of the Department of State for Miscellaneous and Contingent Expenses, Feb. 1, 1798–Nov. 3, 1820, microcopy T-903, National Archives. Although the print purchased by the State Department is not otherwise specified, the date of the entry and the price of the print seem sufficient to establish this as the print published by Carey.

[50]Thomas Jefferson, *Notes on the State of Virginia* ("First Hot-Pressed Edition," Philadelphia, June 1801).

C. Bouch del.t Déposé à la Bibliothèque Nationale le 27 fructidor an 9. Aug.te Desnoyers Sculp.t

THOMAS JEFFERSON.

Président des Etats unis de l'Amerique an 1801.

Se trouve chez le C. Martin, C.d M.d d'Estampes, Rue Fossés Montmartre N.o 27.

ferson for Augustus Day a short time afterward.[51] The most important use of Tiebout's engraving published by Carey, however, was that made of it in France, where Auguste Desnoyers published an engraving in Paris in September 1801. An early work of Desnoyers,[52] who became one of the most eminent engravers of his time, the engraving was taken from a crayon drawing by Bouch made in 1801.[53] Bouch's drawing, in turn, had been taken from Tiebout's engraving.[54] Where Bouch made his copy or how it got into the hands of Desnoyers is unknown, but Desnoyers acknowledged his indebtedness to Bouch on the plate, which is signed "Bouch delt. Aug. Desnoyers Sculpt." The plate also bears the inscription: "Thomas Jefferson. President des Etats unis de l'Amerique an 1801" (fig. 27). Desnoyers's engraving became the major source for the image of Jefferson that was known in France.

[51] See p. 67 below.

[52] Jean Adhémar and Jacques Lethève, *Inventaire du Fonds Français après 1800* (Paris: Bibliothèque Nationale, 1953), p. 421.

[53] Thieme and Becker identify an English artist named Bouch who drew the portrait of Admiral John Jervis, earl of St. Vincent, in Lisbon in 1797, now in the National Portrait Gallery, London (Ulrich Thieme and Felix Becker, eds., *Allgemeines Lexikon der Bildenden Künstler von der Antike bis zur Gegenwart* [Leipzig, 1910], 4: 425). It seems probable that this was the artist whose drawing was the source of Desnoyers's engraving.

[54] Bush, "Life Portraits of Jefferson," p. 57.

Fig. 27. Thomas Jefferson. Engraving by Auguste Desnoyers, Paris, 1801

CHAPTER IV

A Rivalry of Full-Length Prints

OF ALL THE ENGRAVED PRINTS OF JEFFERSON THAT appeared during his presidency, two full-length portraits published in 1801 were in size and design the most ambitious. They were also the most extensively advertised of any Jefferson likenesses and the objects of the greatest public competition among publishers of Jefferson prints.

On September 8, 1800, George Helmbold, Jr., of Philadelphia announced plans for publishing a "full length portrait of Thomas Jefferson, Esquire." In newspaper advertisements that appeared repeatedly over the next nine months, he specified the following conditions:

> 1. The engraving will be done from a Portrait of this American Patriot, taken expressly for the purpose by an eminent Portrait painter — and will be executed by an Engraver of the first rate abilities.
>
> 2. The size of the Print shall be 22 inches in length and 14 inches in breadth, so as to make it a match for Stuart's print of Gen. WASHINGTON.
>
> 3. The price to Subscribers will be Six Dollars. The price to non-subscribers will be enhanced.

4. The subscription money to be paid on the delivery of the Print, which is expected to take place in five months.

5. The publisher pledges himself that the Likeness shall be accurate and striking, and that the engraving shall be equal, if not superior to any work of the kind hitherto executed in the United States.

Subscriptions received by the publisher, No. 72 Race-street, and by his agents throughout the United States.[1]

When the notice was reprinted on the following day, an addendum announced that "a specimen of the engraver's abilities, may be seen at the publisher's, or at the Aurora office. — Also, of the painting will be added in a few days."

After running this advertisement in the Philadelphia *Aurora* three times a week for several months, Helmbold on December 17 altered the notice to indicate that a specimen of the painting could now be seen and added that "upon mature deliberation, G. Helmbold postpones the publication of Mr. BURR'S Portrait."[2] By this date it was known that the electoral vote in the presidential election had resulted in a tie between Jefferson and Burr;[3] and, although Jefferson had plainly been the Republican candidate for president and Burr just as clearly the vice-presidential nominee, it was up to the House of Representatives to resolve the tie. Publisher Helmbold made it clear where he stood in the rising controversy.

In a notice dated January 26, 1801, Helmbold informed the patrons of his portrait of "THE MAN OF THE PEOPLE" that the work had been "in the engraver's hands for a length of time, and that proof sheets may shortly be seen." He continued: "The publisher

[1] *Aurora* (Philadelphia), Sept. 8, 1800, advertisement dated Sept. 8.

[2] Ibid., Dec. 17, 1800.

[3] The news of the outcome of the election in South Carolina, the last state to decide its electoral vote, reached Washington on Dec. 12, 1800 (see Jefferson to Henry Knox, Mar. 27, 1801, Paul L. Ford, ed., *The Writings of Thomas Jefferson*, 10 vols., [New York, 1892–99], 8: 36–37).

intreats the public not to *patronize any other undertaking*, of the same nature, until they have had an opportunity of judging of the merit of his; he hopes he will be indulged in this request, *by every candid republican*, when they learn that he was the first who made proposals for the work, and was only prevented from having the print published already by the chicane and villainy of a few persons; it is not necessary to name them, as their feelings, if they are not too much inured to malpractices will inform them who I mean." Helmbold also announced that "a copy of the painting may be seen at Mr. J. Brown's, No. 129 Chesnut, near Fourth Streets," and that the engraved print would be available "framed and glazed in a style of neatness and elegance for 12 dollars."[4]

Some readers must have suspected that Helmbold's attack referred to the portrait of Jefferson published by Mathew Carey dated February 20, 1801, for on February 28, "to prevent misconception," Helmbold added a sentence to his advertisement in the *Aurora* insisting that his statement regarding improper conduct had "no reference or allusion whatsoever to Mr. Carey, or his recent publication of a *bust portrait* of Mr. Jefferson."[5] Just what "chicane and villainy" Helmbold was protesting is not clear, but the publisher of the competing print was Augustus Day, who began running the following advertisement, dated February 20, in the *Aurora* on February 23, 1801:

> THOMAS JEFFERSON
> DEDICATED TO THE FIRM SUPPORTERS OF
> THEIR COUNTRY.
>
> NOW publishing by AUGUSTUS DAY, No. 38 Chesnut-Street, opposite Mr. Ormrod's Book-store, a whole length Portrait of THOMAS JEFFERSON. The painting is executed in a masterly style by Rembrendt; the engraving is in a state of forwardness and is executing by Mr. Tiebout, an American artist of the first abilities.

[4] *Aurora*, Feb. 26, 27, 1801.

[5] Ibid., Feb. 28, 1801.

> Mr. Jefferson is represented as a philosopher and statesman, holding in one hand the Declaration of Independence; to his right on the table stands a bust of Franklin, and to his left a philosophical apparatus — which, together renders the work highly interesting.
>
> The painting is exhibiting at the above store, where the terms will be made known, and a book open for subscription.[6]

For the next four months, the competing advertisements of Day and Helmbold appeared in the *Aurora*, frequently on the same page.[7] On April 3, Helmbold announced that his print would be ready for delivery in a few days. "A comment upon its excellence for execution, similitude, or elegance, would be superfluous," he extolled. "It need only be seen to meet the approbation of the most refined connisseur." He instructed readers that a copy of the painting could be seen at David Kennedy's at the corner of Market and Seventh streets in Philadelphia.[8] Despite Helmbold's promise, April passed without his print appearing.

By early May, Augustus Day had proof sheets of his work available, and Helmbold renewed his attack. In a notice published in the New York *American Citizen*, May 5, 1801, he cautioned readers not to subscribe to Day's print, "as it is the opinion of men intimately acquainted with Mr. J. that it is absolutely necessary to write under the Painting the Name of Mr. Jefferson, to inform the spectator who it is intended for." He accused "Day and his gang of

[6]Ibid., Feb. 23, 1801. Rembrandt Peale announced in a notice appearing in the *Pennsylvania Packet* (Philadelphia), Dec. 4, 1800, that because few persons discriminated between the names of his father, uncle, brother, and himself, he would be known only by his first name "Rembrandt" (notice reprinted in Prime, ed., *Arts and Crafts in Philadelphia, Maryland, and South Carolina*, pp. 25–26).

[7]See, for example, issues of May 2, 6, 1801.

[8]*Aurora*, April 7, 15, 1801, advertisement dated April 3; also published in the *Republican* (Petersburg), April 30, 1801. Later publications of this advertisement indicated that a copy of the painting could be seen at the office of the *Aurora* (*Aurora*, April 28, June 2, 1801).

associates" of hurrying the print along in order to get the first sales from "those who, not knowing Mr. Jefferson's features correctly, would be led to believe it a semblance."[9]

Much of Helmbold's attack on Day was based on his resentment that it was "unfair and ungentlemanlike" for Day to begin a competing print after he had announced his publication plans.[10] In a notice dated Philadelphia, May 6, 1801, addressed to potential purchasers in the Norfolk, Virginia, area, Helmbold explained at length:

> In September last I issued proposals for publishing a full length portrait of the present PRESIDENT of the United States, and began the work in November following. While our prospects of success in the presidential election were very brilliant, a person heretofore obscure and whose republicanism is very doubtful, of the name of Augustus Day, began to entertain ideas of publishing a portrait upon a plan nearly similar to mine. . . . On the receipt of the result of the election in South Carolina, he issued proposals and began the work, and by hurrying it on at hap hazard has been able to present to the public proof sheets of what he calls a portrait of Mr. Jefferson. I have heard the opinions of men of taste, which do not dispose me to think very favorable of the design, execution or semblance, nor to be apprehensive of its proving injurious to me with men of taste, who are in the least acquainted with Mr. Jefferson's features.
>
> My motives for this publication are to assert my right of priority, which is ever respected by every man of honor, and to caution the inhabitants of Norfolk and its vicinity against mistaking Day's publication for mine.[11]

In this notice Helmbold also stated that his engraving would be executed by David Edwin, "whose abilities were well known in the line of his profession."

[9] *American Citizen*, May 5, 8, 1801. Another notice by Helmbold about Day's print appeared in the *American Citizen*, May 9, 11, 12, 13, 1801 (Gottesman, *Arts and Crafts in New York, 1800–1804*, p. 57).

[10] *American Citizen*, May 5, 8, 1801.

[11] *Epitome of the Times* (Norfolk), June 5, 12, 16, 23, 1801.

Financial pressures undoubtedly explain much of the sharp tone of Helmbold's attacks on Day. In April 1801 he applied directly to President Jefferson for an appointment, particularly the position of purveyor of public supplies, an officer stationed in Philadelphia. In his letter of application, he described himself as the editor of a Philadelphia German gazette that was having difficulty because of the rapid decline in the use of the German language. "Some few months ago I was in hopes of my not being necessiated to make any application for an Appointment," he explained, "from the prospect of success I had in view from publishing a full length portrait of yourself; but those prospects have in a great degree be[en] rendered a nullity or illusion from another person setting up one in opposition to me, so that I shall merely clear whatever I may have expended." He assured the president that he had "uniformly supported the republican cause," but he did not receive any appointment.[12]

The announcements that Helmbold issued in early May reported that his print would "positively be published" in the course of the month.[13] However, it was not until June 16 that he promised subscribers that their prints "will be delivered in the course of the week." To compensate them for their long wait Helmbold gave each subscriber a copy of his recently published pamphlet *A Concise Account of the Life of the President of the United States*.[14] Finally, on July 4, 1801, the *Aurora* carried an advertisement dated July 2 that "this day is published, by George Helmbold, Junior, . . . a full length portrait of Thomas Jefferson, President of the United States" (fig. 28; see also fig. 29). Helmbold continued: "The pub-

[12]George Helmbold, Jr., to Jefferson, April 3, 7, 1801, Letters of Application and Recommendation, RG 59, National Archives. Helmbold was publisher of the *Neue Philadelphische Correspondenz* (Clarence S. Brigham, *History and Bibliography of American Newspapers, 1690–1820*, 2 vols. [Worcester, Mass., 1947], 2: 927).

[13]Advertisement dated May 6, *Epitome of the Times*, June 5, 1801. See also *American Citizen*, May 8, 1801.

[14]*Aurora*, July 9, 1801.

Fig. 28. Thomas Jefferson. Engraving by David Edwin, published by George Helmbold, Jr., Philadelphia, 1801

Fig. 29. Thomas Jefferson. Engraving (second state) by David Edwin, published by George Helmbold, Jr., Philadelphia, 1801

lisher deems it unnecessary to offer any praise upon this publication, the approbation which it has already received from the best judges, for correctness and excellent execution, assure him of its meeting with the most distinguished patronage from the friends of arts, and a liberal and discerning public."[15]

In addition to being sold at two Helmbold shops in Philadelphia and at the office of the *Aurora*, the print was available for sale in sixteen other cities from Bennington, Vermont, to Savannah, Georgia, including all of the largest cities — Boston, New York, Baltimore, Charleston, and Richmond — and most of the lesser ones — Albany, New London, Hartford, Portsmouth, N.H., Washington, D.C., Alexandria, Petersburg, Norfolk, and Raleigh.[16] Most of the agents were publishers of Republican newspapers. Some of them had been carrying Helmbold's earlier announcements of the forthcoming publication of the print,[17] and many of them now advertised the arrival of the print. The Baltimore *American* carried the following advertisement:

> JEFFERSON
>
> Subscriptions received for the elegantly engraved and striking likeness of THOMAS JEFFERSON, President of the U. States, pub-

[15] Ibid., July 4, 10, 1801.

[16] The prints were sold by the following dealers: David Denniston and James Cheetham, New York; John Barber, Albany; Charles Holt, New London, Conn.; Elisha Babcock, Hartford; Abijah Adams and Ebenezer Rhoades, Boston; Samuel Nutting and John Whitelock, Portsmouth, N.H.; Anthony Haswell, Bennington, Vt.; Vincent Bonsal and Hezekiah Niles, Baltimore; Samuel Harrison Smith, Washington, D.C.; Thomas Cruse, Alexandria; Meriwether Jones, Richmond; Thomas Field, Petersburg; Augustus C. Jordan, Norfolk; Joseph Gales, Raleigh; John McIver and David R. Williams, Charleston; Dr. Love, Savannah (ibid., July 4, 1801).

[17] *Independent Chronicle* (Boston), Mar. 9, 23, 30, April 13, 20, 1801; *American* (Baltimore), Mar. 24, 26, April 1, 1801; *American Citizen* (New York), April 4, 6, 7, 8, 9, 20, 21, 25, 1801; *Epitome of the Times* (Norfolk), Nov. 6, 10, Dec. 1, 8, 1800, Jan. 2, 16, 30, Feb. 3, 17, 20, 24, 27, Mar. 3, 10, 17, 1801.

> lished by HELMBOLD, either in sheets, or superbly framed, by THOMAS LEAMAN, Cumberland Row, or at the Office of the American; where specimens of the work are exhibited.[18]

The widespread distribution of this print of Jefferson can thus be well documented. Although no dealers west of the mountains were listed by Helmbold, the print had extensive distribution in the coastal states and received considerable newspaper publicity.

Augustus Day also chose July 4, 1801, as the day on which to announce his "just published" whole-length portrait of Jefferson (fig. 30),[19] and the competition between Helmbold and Day continued. An advertisement in the Charleston, South Carolina, *City-Gazette* announcing the Helmbold print vehemently attacked the Day publication. Affirming that "merit will maintain its right in despite of opposition in an unfair manner," the notice continued:

> The subscribers and others, are also informed, (as per New-York papers) that Mssrs. Tiebout and Day, of Philadelphia have just published a full length Print of Jefferson; 'tis a very poor copy stolen from the original picture, in the possession of Mr. Helmbold, by an engraver of no merit, and published with an idea of injuring Helmbold's; but the shortness of the time in which they were doing it, with many other concurring circumstances, convinces us that it is a catch-penny thing, and rather a caracature on the Patriot, than otherwise.[20]

The Helmbold print appeared in two versions (see figs. 28 and 29), which were published so closely together as to suggest that the first print may have been rushed to completion to be ready for publication on the Fourth of July 1801 in order not to permit the competing Day print to appear first. A notice dated June 24, 1801, advertising the Helmbold print, informed readers of the Charleston

[18] Advertisement dated July 23, *American*, Aug. 18, 19, 21, 22, 1801. See also *American Citizen*, July 21, 1801.

[19] Advertisement dated July 4, *Aurora*, July 4, 1801.

[20] Advertisement dated June 24, *City-Gazette and Daily Advertiser* (Charleston), July 13, 1801.

Fig. 30. Thomas Jefferson. Engraving by Cornelius Tiebout, published by Augustus Day, Philadelphia, 1801

City-Gazette that "the publication has been delayed two or three weeks, owing to that eminent Artist Gabriel Steward's making such improvements in the likeness and disposition of the Picture, as he thought necessary, which will render the print equal to his full length Washington, for which the Jefferson is meant as a fellow Picture."[21]

No evidence has been found to show that Gilbert Stuart had any connection with Helmbold's print, but it is of interest that Helmbold appealed to Jefferson in May 1801 for aid in relief of "the celebrated Portrait Painter" at a time when Stuart's property was being attached for debts.[22] Moreover, in July 1801, with his first Jefferson print finally out, Helmbold announced that "encouraged by the patronage he has lately experienced," he planned to publish "a series of the most distinguished public characters in America" and "has been so fortunate to prevail upon Mr. *Gilbert Stuart*, to furnish the series of Paintings, and Mr. David Edwin to execute the engravings under his direction." Jefferson was to be included among the new prints.[23] This series, like the one announced by Stuart a year earlier, was never published, but there was obviously some contact between Helmbold and Stuart at the time he was revising his plate. When Helmbold announced the publication of the revised print on September 14, 1801, however, he gave no hint of any involvement by Stuart but rather advertised that his full-length portrait of Jefferson, "having undergone several material alterations as suggested by Amateurs, is now acknowledged to be the best Likeness ever published."[24]

Despite his aspersions on the inferiority of his rival's print, Helmbold's publication of a revised print was prompted, it may be argued, by the superiority of Day's print. Engraved by Cornelius

[21] Ibid.

[22] George Helmbold, Jr., to Jefferson, May 12, 1801, Jefferson Papers, Lib. Cong.

[23] *Aurora*, July 10, 1801.

[24] Advertisement dated Sept. 14, ibid., Sept. 15, 1801.

Tiebout, Day's plate depicts Jefferson surrounded by those things that interested and described him. He is shown displaying the Declaration of Independence, with a bust of Franklin on a table to his right, and a static electrical machine to his left (see fig. 30).[25] In David Edwin's first plate published by Helmbold, a rather squatty figure stands holding a glove in his right hand and resting his left hand on a globe of the world (see fig. 28). Edwin's materially altered plate shows a taller and slimmer Jefferson and adds a chair at Jefferson's right (see fig. 29). Despite Helmbold's earlier criticism that it was necessary for Day to put Jefferson's name under the portrait to identify the subject, Helmbold's second plate is inscribed "Jefferson."

Since both Tiebout and Edwin had previously engraved portraits of Jefferson from Rembrandt Peale's painting, each engraver copied his previous work in engraving the head for his full-length portrait. The head of Jefferson in Tiebout's plate for Day is a close copy of his engraving for Mathew Carey (see fig. 25). Edwin's copy for Helmbold follows less closely his 1800 engraving of Jefferson as vice-president (see fig. 7), but that source can be recognized in the full-length engraving.

Although nothing is known about the financial success of either the Helmbold or the Day print, Helmbold's print continued to be extensively advertised. The Norfolk *Epitome of the Times* announced in October 1801 that "Mr. Eastwick has just arrived in town from Philadelphia, with *Helmbold's full length Portrait of Jefferson*, in elegant gilt frames of various sizes. This impression has been taken since the late improvements in the plate, notice of which was some time ago given in the public prints."[26]

[25] The American Philosophical Society had such a machine in its collection (see Robert P. Multhauf, comp., *A Catalogue of Instruments and Models in the Possession of the American Philosophical Society* [Philadelphia, 1961], pp. 119–20 and frontispiece).

[26] *Epitome of the Times*, Oct. 9, 13, 1801. For other advertisements of Helmbold's print, see *Republican* (Petersburg), Sept. 17, 23, Oct. 5, 9, 15, 26, Nov. 5, Dec. 3, 7, 1801; *Examiner* (Richmond), Dec. 22, 25, 1801.

Day's print later became the subject of a lawsuit that he brought against John Wesley Jarvis, a young engraver and printseller in New York, later to become a successful portrait painter.[26] The case began in the Philadelphia County Court of Common Pleas in September 1805, when Day sought compensation from Jarvis for failing to carry out an earlier agreement to exchange fifty of James Heath's engravings of Washington for fifty of Day's prints of Jefferson. (Both prints were priced to subscribers at $5.25, with a trade discount of 25 percent.) Although Day had sent Jarvis fifty Jefferson prints, Jarvis supplied Day with only twenty-five Washington prints in exchange, refusing to provide more on the ground that the Jefferson print had declined in value, while the Washington print was still in demand. When the case came to trial in January 1808, Jarvis's counsel denied the existence of a contract, and went on to argue that:

> whatever the artist might have intended, the "*Jeffersons*" were never considered matches for "*Washingtons*," by any persons of the least taste or judgment: that although a few of the "*Jeffersons*" were put off, at the subscription price, soon after publication, and had a tolerable brisk sale, yet that the moment they were submitted to the test of criticism, and were compared with the "*Washingtons*," they were condemned by the unbiassed judgment of the public, and fell, as he was able to prove by a deposition, which he held in his hand (but which being *ex parte*, he was not permitted to read) to twelve and thirteen cents apiece, by wholesale, and at that price *were a dull article*; and that to him it appeared monstrous that when the plaintiff had found a ready sale, and received a full price for the twenty-five "*Washingtons*," exceeding the value of all the "*Jeffersons*," that were ever turned from his plate, he should at this time come forward, and demand the same price for his "*Jeffersons*," which began to depreciate before they were dry from the press, and were now *of less value than waste paper*.[28]

[27] See Harold E. Dickson, "Day vs. Jarvis," *Pennsylvania Magazine of History and Biography* 63 (1939): 169–88.

[28] John E. Hall, ed., *The American Law Journal and Miscellaneous Repertory* 1 (1808): 176.

The jury decided in favor of Day, ordering Jarvis to compensate him for the twenty-five Jefferson prints for which he had received nothing in exchange.[29] Whatever the popularity of Jefferson prints may have been at the time of the embargo, when the case was settled, Day's print must have had more success than Jarvis's lawyer was willing to concede, for it was reissued twice by other Philadelphia print publishers.[30]

If neither Tiebout in engraving the plate for Day nor Edwin in either version of his plate for Helmbold succeeded in capturing the presence of Jefferson, it should be noted that neither engraver had a full-length portrait of Jefferson taken from life to copy. In fact, only in Trumbull's *Declaration of Independence* had Jefferson been shown standing, and that painting was not known to either engraver in 1801. Although both Tiebout and Edwin might have seen Jefferson in Philadelphia, neither was able to transfer successfully his impression to a copperplate. No artist was to draw a full-length portrait of Jefferson from life during his presidential years, and no other engraver attempted a full-length plate, thus leaving the prints by Tiebout and Edwin as the only such efforts to reach the public.

[29] Day was awarded damages of $118.12 (ibid.).

[30] Day's plate was republished by W. H. Morgan, Philadelphia, and later by William Smith, 702 South Third Street, Philadelphia (see cat. no. 22 below). The dates for these prints have not been determined, but it seems likely that Morgan reprinted the Jefferson plate in connection with the plans he announced, Feb. 28, 1809, to publish a whole-length portrait of Madison engraved by David Edwin "to correspond with those already published of presidents Washington and Jefferson" (*Aurora*, Mar. 2, 1809).

CHAPTER V

Two Medallic Portraits

IN APRIL 1802 JEFFERSON WROTE TO HIS DAUGHTER Martha: "I inclose you a medal executed by an artist lately from Europe and who appears to be equal to any in the world. It is taken from Houdon's bust, for he never saw me. It sells the more readily as the prints which have been offered the public are such miserable caracatures."[1] About the same time, Congressman Samuel L. Mitchill of New York was writing to his wife that he had "procured a fine and elegant Silver Medal of the President of the U.S." After sending it to her, Mitchill responded to his wife's acknowledgment by writing: "I am glad you are pleased with the Jefferson Medal. Is it not elegant? The likeness is striking."[2]

Martha Jefferson Randolph also found the medal pleasing, telling to her father: "I received with gratitude and pleasure unexpressible, my dearest Father, the elegant medal you sent me. It arrived

[1]Jefferson to Martha Jefferson Randolph, April 3, 1802, Edwin Morris Betts and James Adam Bear, Jr., eds., *The Family Letters of Thomas Jefferson* (Columbia, Mo., 1966), p. 221. Jefferson also sent his daughter Maria one of the medals (Jefferson to Mary [Maria] Jefferson Eppes, Mar. 29, 1802, ibid., pp. 220–21).

[2]Samuel L. Mitchill to his wife, Mar. 3, April 1, 1802, Mitchill Papers, Museum of the City of New York.

safely with out a scratch even, and is I think a good likeness; but as I found fault with Houdon for making you too old I shall have the same quarrel with the medal also. You have many years to live before the likeness can be a perfect one."[3]

What was this medal that both Representative Mitchill and Martha Jefferson Randolph described as elegant and that obviously met the approval of Jefferson himself? The answer can be found in an advertisement which appeared in the Philadelphia *Aurora*, February 20, 1802, announcing:

> A STRIKING LIKENESS
> of
> THOMAS JEFFERSON,
> PRESIDENT OF THE U. STATES;
>
> ON a *Medallion*, executed by Mr. Reish, the celebrated German Artist, to commemorate, at once, the Era of American Independence, and the auspicious day, which raised Mr. JEFFERSON, to the dignity of President over a free people.
>
> On the reverse of this elegant medallion, are represented emblematical figures, in a style of workmanship never equalled before in this country, and excelled in none.
>
> It will depend upon the encouragement Mr. Reish meets with, in this first exhibition of his talents in this country, whether he will reside in America, or return to Europe. The patriots who wish to preserve the remembrance of American independence, and the elevation of Thomas Jefferson, as well as to retain a valuable artist, may be supplied with medallions on Silver or White Metal, at the *Aurora* Book-Store, and no where else in Philadelphia.[4]

The medal was priced at $4.25 in silver and $1.25 in white metal (pewter). It is 45 millimeters in diameter.

On the obverse of the medal Jefferson is shown in profile from Houdon's bust, with the inscription: "TH. JEFFERSON PRESIDENT OF THE U.S. 4 MARCH 1801" (fig. 31). The portrait was signed by

[3] Martha Jefferson Randolph to Jefferson, April 16, 1802, Betts and Bear, eds., *Family Letters of Thomas Jefferson*, p. 222.

[4] Advertisement dated Feb. 17, *Aurora*, Feb. 20, 1802.

Fig. 31. Obverse of medal engraved by John Reich, Philadelphia, 1802

Fig. 32. Reverse of medal engraved by John Reich, Philadelphia, 1802

John Reich with the initials "*JR*." On the reverse the goddess of liberty, holding the Declaration of Independence in her hand, stands by a rock inscribed "Constitution." An eagle bearing a wreath hovers above. The legend reads: "UNDER HIS WING IS PROTECTION," and in exergue: "TO COMMEMORATE JULY 4 1776" (fig. 32).

Surprisingly, except among numismatists, the medal is little known today,[5] yet it was widely available in Jefferson's day and could be purchased in pewter for less than the price of many of the engraved prints that Jefferson regarded as caricatures. How many Americans took advantage of this opportunity to procure a likeness of the president is not known, but those admirers who purchased this commemorative medal as a souvenir of his inauguration were rewarded not only with a handsome medal but also with an unusually good likeness.

Closely resembling the medal by Reich celebrating Jefferson's inauguration was the Indian peace medal issued in 1801. This was the first of the Indian medals to show the head of an American president. The figure of Washington had been engraved on some of the medals given to Indian leaders during his presidency, but neither Washington's head nor that of Adams had appeared in the

[5] It has been pictured and described in Robert James Eidlitz, "Medals Relating to Thomas Jefferson," *The Numismatist* 37 (1924): 525–26, and in Melvin Fuld, "Some Medals of Thomas Jefferson," ibid., 83 (1970): 24. It is also included in Neil MacNeil, *The President's Medal, 1789–1977* (New York, 1977), p. 18.

manner of European monarchs on these medals that were treasured by, and symbolically important to, Indian chiefs as marks of status, loyalty, and friendship. No record has been found to indicate who was responsible for the change in the medals or whether Jefferson had any part in the new design, but that the Indians reacted favorably to the representation of the Great Father is suggested by the fact that all succeeding American peace medals bore on the obverse the portrait of the president.[6]

In June 1801 Elias Boudinot, the director of the United States Mint in Philadelphia, wrote to Jefferson: "I have been waited on by Mr. Reich and was much pleased with the samples of his work. He has been liberated from his servitude by means of one of the officers of the mint; since which I have set him to work on a particular medal, to be ascertained of his abilities. I am obliged to use great precaution, in regard to employing him in the mint, before I can have good evidence of the integrity of his character."[7] It may be that the medal referred to here was the Indian peace medal, but this has not been established. However, that Reich was the engraver who designed that medal is supported by his well-documented execution of the Jefferson inaugural medal which closely resembles the Indian medal and by his clear association with the mint at the time the Indian peace medal was being designed.[8]

[6]Francis Paul Prucha, *Indian Peace Medals in American History* (Madison, Wis., 1971), p. 90; Francis Paul Prucha, "American Indian Peace Medals," *Chicago History* 2 (1972): 106–9.

[7]Boudinot to Jefferson, June 16, 1801, Jefferson Papers, Lib. Cong.

[8]Prucha in *Indian Peace Medals* questions the identification of Reich as the designer of the medal and credits it to Robert Scott, the engraver at the mint, though he admits the unlikely possibility that Reich may have worked on the medal under Scott's direction (pp. 91, 95). The probability that the work was contracted out to Reich, however, seems likely, particularly in light of a letter from Robert Patterson, director of the mint in 1807, to Jefferson concerning appointing Reich as assistant engraver. Patterson wrote that "if this

The Jefferson Indian peace medal was struck in three sizes, requiring three pairs of dies for the three medals and producing minor variations in the portraits in each size. While the images are remarkably close, the smallest of the three most nearly resembles the medal celebrating Jefferson's inauguration. The latter medal is 45 millimeters; the smallest of the Indian peace medals is 54–55 millimeters. The largest of the Indian medals is 101–5 millimeters; the middle size measures 76–77 millimeters. Variations in the size of the individual medals resulted from the manner in which the medals were made. Because of their large size, the two sides of the medals were struck separately on thin sheets of silver, then united by a silver band or rim, to which a ring for suspension was attached at the top.[9] The largest size was the largest medal struck at the United States Mint and is particularly impressive, but the likenesses of Jefferson on all examples of the medal are striking. All are inscribed: "TH. JEFFERSON PRESIDENT OF THE U.S. A.D. 1801" (fig. 33). On the reverse the inscription "PEACE AND FRIENDSHIP" is symbolized by a crossed tomahawk and peace pipe and by clasped hands. On the wrist of one hand a silver band, such as worn by Indian chiefs, is embossed with an American eagle. The braided cuff of a United States military uniform shows above the other hand (fig. 34).

---

gentleman should be employed, perhaps more than his salary would be saved to the publick, in what is usually expended on the engraving of dies for medals; but which might then be executed by an artist in their own service, with little or no additional expence." This strongly suggests that Reich may previously have been employed by the mint in a contractual arrangement. After Reich was hired, Patterson also wrote to Jefferson that "if any seals should be wanted for the public offices, or dies for the striking of Indian or other medals, they can now be executed in the best state, at the mint, without any extra expence to government" (Patterson to Jefferson, Mar. 25, April 3, 1807, Jefferson Papers, Lib. Cong.).

[9]Prucha, *Indian Peace Medals*, p. 91; Bauman L. Belden, *Indian Peace Medals Issued in the United States* (New Milford, Conn., 1966), pp. 24–25.

Fig. 33. Obverse of Indian peace medal, engraved by John Reich, 1801

Fig. 34. Reverse of Indian peace medal, engraved by John Reich, 1801

The War Department, which administered Indian affairs, received its first shipment of Jefferson peace medals from the mint in December 1801. On the initial order 168 medals were produced at a cost of nearly $1,300. In the course of Jefferson's presidency hundreds more of the medals were manufactured, although the exact number has not been determined. Records relating to their purchase and distribution, however, leave no doubt that large numbers of the Jefferson medals were distributed to Indian chiefs not only by military officers and Indian commissioners at the signing of treaties but also by Indian agents on the frontier. The purveyor of public supplies in Philadelphia purchased 220 Jefferson medals for "Presents to the Indians" between November 1805 and August 1806. Records of the distribution of these medals show that Governor William Hull at Detroit in May 1806 received 10 large-size Jefferson medals, 12 middle-size, and 16 small-size. Pierre Chouteau at St. Louis in June 1806 received 36 Jefferson medals, 12 in each of the three sizes; and the United States factor at the Arkansas Post, John B. Treat, in July 1806 received 22 Jefferson medals in different sizes.[10]

Meriwether Lewis and William Clark took a supply of the medals on their great expedition to the Pacific and presented them to Indian chiefs in accordance with their importance. Records of the expedition show that they carried with them three large-size Jeffer-

[10] Prucha, *Indian Peace Medals*, pp. 91, 94.

son medals, thirteen of the second size, and sixteen of the third size.[11] At the first presentation ceremony, as recorded in their journals, they sent a flag and a medal to the "principal Chief" of the Oto and Missouri nation and gave "a medal of Second Grade" to one Oto chief, the same to one Missouri chief, and "4 medals of a third Grade to the inferior chiefs two for each tribe."[12] In presenting the new medals of the president, Lewis and Clark also called upon Indian leaders to turn in "all the flags and medals which you may have received from your old fathers the French and Spaniards, or from any other nation whatever, your father will give you new flags and new medals of his own in exchange. . . . It is not proper since you have become the children of the great chief of the Seventeen great nations of America, that you should wear or keep those emblems of attachment to any other great father but himself."[13]

After a delegation of Indian "Chiefs from the Missouri and Mississippi" arrived in Washington in December 1805, they were given uniforms and medals; and they were soon wearing both. "Some had the likeness of Jefferson, engraved on silver, I believe, hanging at their breasts," one observer reported.[14] When they reached Boston, Governor Caleb Strong presented them with silver chains for wearing their Jefferson medals.[15] Drawing portraits

[11] In addition, they carried 55 smaller medals struck at the time of Washington's presidency. These were the so-called season medals made in three designs — a man sowing grain, domestic animals, and women spinning and weaving (ibid., p. 17).

[12] Entry for Aug. 3, 1804, Reuben Gold Thwaites, ed., *Original Journals of the Lewis and Clark Expedition, 1804–1806*, 8 vols. (New York, 1904–5), 1: 97.

[13] Lewis and Clark to the Oto Indians, [Aug. 4, 1804], Donald Jackson, ed., *Letters of the Lewis and Clark Expedition, with Related Documents, 1783–1854* (Urbana, Ill., 1962), p. 208.

[14] *Aurora*, Jan. 28, 1806.

[15] John C. Ewers, "'Chiefs from the Missouri and Mississippi' and Peale's Silhouettes of 1806," *Smithsonian Journal of History* 1 (1966): 12–22.

of the Indian leaders during their Washington visit, Saint-Mémin sketched Payouska, the chief of the Great Osage, wearing his Jefferson medal.[16]

It is not surprising that the Indian chiefs prized the handsome medals, though at times of conflict some defiantly discarded them.[17] It is of no little interest that of all Americans who acquired an image of President Jefferson, the Indian leaders possessed a likeness that was unexcelled in correctness and elegance.

[16]The drawing is reproduced in Luke V. Lockwood, "The St. Memin Indian Portraits," *New-York Historical Society Quarterly Bulletin* 12 (1928): 4.

[17]See Nathaniel Pryor to William Clark, Oct. 16, 1807, Jackson, ed., *Letters of the Lewis and Clark Expedition*, pp. 433–35.

CHAPTER VI

The Presidential Profile by Saint-Mémin

BY THE TIME OF JEFFERSON'S ELECTION TO THE PRESidency, Charles-Balthazar-Julien Févret de Saint-Mémin, a young French émigré artist who had come to the United States in 1793, had established himself as the preeminent master of the physiognotrace invented in France by Gilles-Louis Chrétien. Saint-Mémin worked first mainly in New York, but in 1798 he moved to Philadelphia and later traveled about to other cities before returning to France in 1814.[1] An advertisement appearing in the Philadelphia *Aurora* early in 1799 announced:

> PHISIOGNOTRACE.
> *Likenesses Engraved.*
> The subscriber begs leave to inform the public that he takes and engraves portraits on an improved plan of the celebrated phisiognotrace of Paris, and in a style never introduced before in this country.

[1]Fillmore Norfleet, *Saint-Mémin in Virginia: Portraits and Biographies* (Richmond, 1942), pp. 13–15, 23; Howard C. Rice, Jr., "Saint-Mémin's Portrait of Jefferson," *Princeton University Library Chronicle* 20 (1959): 182; see also Elias Dexter, *The St.-Mémin Collections of Portraits; Consisting of Seven Hundred and Sixty Medallion Portraits, Principally of Distinguished Americans* (New York, 1862).

> A great number of portraits of distinguished persons, who honoured the artist with their patronage at New-York, may be seen at S. Chaudron's, No. 12, South Third street, or at the subscriber's, No. 32, South Third street. He delivers with the original portrait, the plate engraved, and twelve copies of the same.
>
> St. MEMIN[2]

With the aid of the physiognotrace, Saint-Mémin drew the outline of a life-size profile on a coarse-textured paper covered with a pink watercolor wash. He then filled in the subject's features and costume with black and white chalk or crayon and gray wash. Using a pantograph, he transferred the profile in reduced size onto a copperplate and engraved the details of the portrait, usually within a circle about two inches in diameter. "The creation of my little engravings is so much my own work," he recalled years later in 1849, "that I was obliged to be at the same time draughtsman and engraver, builder of pantograph, physionotrace, hand-press, manufacturer of *roulettes* and other tools necessary to engraving, brayer of my ink, and, furthermore, my own printer."[3] Saint-Mémin's standard charge was twenty-five dollars for men and thirty-five dollars for women. This included the original portrait, the copperplate, and twelve impressions. Additional prints could be obtained at $1.50 per dozen.[4]

Among those numerous Americans who admired Saint-Mémin's work were Jefferson's two daughters, Martha and Maria, who, learning that Saint-Mémin was going to be in Washington in 1804, appealed to their father to sit for him. Although both daughters wrote to their father on the subject, Maria's letter was the most pleading. She wrote:

> I have a favor to beg of you that I hope will not be refused. It is one which my sister as well as myself is deeply interested in. We had both thought you had promised us your picture if ever St. Mimin went to

[2]*Aurora*, Jan. 8, 1799.

[3]Norfleet, *Saint-Mémin*, pp. 13–14; Bush, "Life Portraits of Jefferson," p. 67.

[4]*Aurora*, Jan. 27, 1801; *Federal Gazette, and Baltimore Daily Advertiser*, May 2, 1803, in Norfleet, *Saint-Mémin*, p. 28.

> Washington. If you did but know what a source of pleasure it would be to us while so much separated from you to have so excellent a likeness of you you would not I think refuse us. It is what we have allways most wanted all our lives and the certainty with which he takes his likenesses makes this one request I think not unreasonable. He will be in Washington the middle of this month and I can not help hoping you will grant us this one favor.[5]

This may have been the last request that Maria made of her father, and it is all the more poignant that Jefferson was unable to fulfill it before he left on April 1 for Monticello, where less than two weeks after his arrival Maria died at the age of twenty-five.[6]

The next time Saint-Mémin set up his physiognotrace in Washington in November 1804,[7] Jefferson carried out his promise. In his account book for November 27, 1804, he recorded: "gave St. Memin order on bk US. for 29.50."[8] This entry is further explained by Saint-Mémin's bill of charges to Jefferson,[9] which specified:

Messr. President to St. Memin	
To a likeness in chalk a plate engraved	
and twelve impressions	$25.00
thirty six extra impressions	4.50
	29.50

Although this statement is undated, it corresponds to the account-book record of November 27, 1804. It is likely that Jefferson made

[5] Mary (Maria) Jefferson Eppes to Jefferson, Feb. 10, [1804], Betts and Bear, eds., *Family Letters of Thomas Jefferson*, pp. 256–57. See also Martha Jefferson Randolph to Jefferson, Jan. 14, 1804, ibid., p. 253.

[6] Dumas Malone, *Jefferson the President: First Term, 1801–1805* (Boston, 1970), pp. 411–15.

[7] Saint-Mémin announced his arrival in Washington in a newspaper advertisement dated Nov. 8, 1804 (*National Intelligencer*, Nov. 12, 14, 16, 1804).

[8] Jefferson, Account Books, transcribed by James A. Bear, Jr., University of Virginia Library.

[9] Undated, endorsed by Jefferson: "St. Memin." St.-Mémin Collection, Prints Division, Lib. Cong.

the payment on the day of the sitting,[10] but even if the sitting and payment were not on the same day, it may be assumed that they were not widely separated and that Jefferson sat for Saint-Mémin in November 1804, the same month that he was reelected president, at age sixty-one.

The small engravings that Jefferson received are signed in the lower left corner "St. Mn. ft." Jefferson's profile is engraved in the form of a round medallion on a copperplate 2 13/16 by 2 5/8 inches (fig. 35).[11] Jefferson presented the prints mainly to his family and relatives, members of the cabinet, and a few friends, including the marquis de Lafayette and the comte de Volney. A list in Jefferson's handwriting names twenty-five persons to whom he gave the profiles.[12] One of the recipients, the comte de Volney, expressed great satisfaction on viewing the miniature, as he called it, and commented that the plumpness of Jefferson's appearance indicated that he had acquired more health.[13] While this round medallion print circulated among Jefferson's friends and relations, a nearly identical portrait, engraved in an oval frame, was available to the public at large.

On February 25, 1805, a week before Jefferson's second inaugural, Saint-Mémin advertised in the Washington *National Intelligencer* that he had "on hand a few likenesses of the President of the United States engraved by himself."[14] It seems certain that these were the oval engravings rather than the round version that Jeffer-

[10] Bush, "Life Portraits of Jefferson," p. 67.

[11] Rice, "Saint-Mémin's Portrait of Jefferson," pp. 183–84. The copperplate is reproduced along with the print in this article.

[12] The list is not labeled, but it is preserved along with two of the Saint-Mémin prints inside a folded paper on the outside of which is written in Jefferson's hand: "Profiles by St. Memin" (Harold Jefferson Coolidge Collection, Jefferson Papers, Univ. of Va. Library, examined with the permission of Harold Jefferson Coolidge).

[13] Volney to Jefferson, July 2, 1805, Jefferson Papers, Lib. Cong.

[14] *National Intelligencer*, Feb. 25, 27, 1805.

Fig. 35. Thomas Jefferson. Mezzotint by Saint-Mémin, 1804

Fig. 36. Thomas Jefferson. Mezzotint by Saint-Mémin, 1805

son received, because the oval print is inscribed "TH: JEFFERSON." Saint-Mémin did not normally put names on the portraits made for individuals themselves. Moreover, although he signed his name in an abbreviated form on the engraving that Jefferson received, he signed the oval engraving "St. Memin delt. & sct." There is little doubt, then, that the oval portrait (fig. 36) was the plate that Saint-Mémin prepared for commercial distribution. It seems equally evident that both the round and the oval engravings came from the same drawing (Appendix, plate V) or that one engraving was copied from the other.[15] Thus, the public had access to the same image of Jefferson that was cherished by his relatives and friends. How widely Saint-Mémin sold the prints, however, cannot be established; no advertisements offering the prints for sale have been found other than in the Washington paper. It is possible that the print offered for sale for one dollar at Duane's Book-Store in Phila-

[15] The assumption by Norfleet (*Saint-Mémin*, pp. 30–31) that Jefferson sat twice for Saint-Mémin was rejected by Kimball ("Life Portraits of Jefferson," p. 523). See also Rice, "Saint-Mémin's Portrait of Jefferson," pp. 186–87.

delphia in April 1805 was Saint-Mémin's print, but it was identified only as "An Admirable Likeness of Thomas Jefferson, President of the United States. Duodecimo size, fit for the parlour or pocket book."[16] The small size of the print suggests Saint-Mémin's plate. Moreover, William Duane would have had access to Saint-Mémin's work through the bookstore he operated in Washington. The evidence is circumstantial, but there is no other engraving known that fits this print advertised in the Philadelphia *Aurora*.

Further evidence of the circulation of Saint-Mémin's portrait can be seen in the apotheosis engraved by Thomas Gimbrede to mark Jefferson's retirement from the presidency (fig. 37). The bust of Jefferson copied from Saint-Mémin was shown by Gimbrede in clouds with Minerva, the goddess of wisdom, above him and a figure of Fame below. The print is inscribed "Thos. Jefferson the Pride of America Retired March 4, 1809."

Two days after Jefferson left office, Gimbrede sent him "a Little Sketch in Cameo . . . as an evidence of my Esteem and high consideration, with an unfeigned wish that in your retirement you may experience that tranquility and happiness that your usefulness in public life has so Eminently entitled you to."[17] In thanking Gimbrede warmly for "the very elegant Cameo," Jefferson wrote: "He considers it as a flattering mark of the indulgence with which Mr. Gimbrede has been so good as to contemplate his public conduct, and it adds to the consolation he receives from the testimony of the worthy that the purity of his intentions, at least, has atoned

[16] *Aurora*, April 27, 29, 30, May 2, 7, 1805.

[17] [Thomas] Gimbrede to Jefferson, Mar. 6, 1809, Jefferson Papers, Lib. Cong. The note was sent from the Union Tavern in Georgetown, and was endorsed by Jefferson: "Gimbrede. Geo.T. Mar. 6. 09 recd. March 6." A misreading of Jefferson's endorsement led the Library of Congress to identify the letter as written by George T. Gimbrede.

Fig. 37. Thomas Jefferson. Engraving by Thomas Gimbrede, New York, 1809

for whatever error he may have involuntarily committed."[18] The two letters leave hardly a doubt that the "Little Sketch in Cameo" refers to Gimbrede's engraved print, and Jefferson's response suggests also that the retiring president, who had just seen his unpopular embargo act repealed, was not displeased to see himself pictured with the goddess of wisdom.

[18] Jefferson to Gimbrede, Mar. 7, 1809, ibid.

CHAPTER VII

The Enduring Jefferson by Gilbert Stuart

UNTIL THE REDISCOVERY OF REMBRANDT PEALE'S original 1800 portrait of Jefferson in 1959 and the public interest in it that followed, the image created by Gilbert Stuart was the predominant icon of Jefferson. Its popularity still widely endures. Stuart's famous image first reached the public late in Jefferson's presidency, when the likeness appeared in an engraving by Robert Field published in Boston, where Stuart was then living. This portrait was soon to supplant Peale's likeness in public popularity.

Jefferson sat for Stuart on three different occasions, which he later described as follows:

> With respect to Mr. Stuart, it was in May, 1800, I got him to draw my picture and immediately after the last sitting I paid him his price, one hundred dollars. He was yet to put the last hand on it, so it was left with him. When he came to Washington in 1805 he told me he was not satisfied with it, and therefore begged me to sit again, and he drew another which he was to deliver me instead of the first, but begged permission to keep it until he could get an engraving from it. I soon after got him to sketch me in the medallion form, which he

> did on paper with crayons. Although a slight thing I gave him another hundred dollars, probably the treble of what he would have asked. This I have; it is a very fine thing, although very perishable.[1]

As indicated earlier, the 1800 portrait to which Jefferson referred has long been lost or may even have been rubbed out by Stuart. Though Stuart announced plans to issue an engraving of it, he never did so; and the engravings that previously have been accepted as deriving from that portrait can be traced, through David Edwin's engraving, to Rembrandt Peale's 1800 portrait.[2] There is no acceptable evidence that Stuart's first portrait was ever engraved. The earliest Stuart likeness of Jefferson to reach the public, therefore, was that of the second life portrait painted in Washington in 1805. That was the likeness copied by Robert Field in his well-executed engraving, which was advertised in the Boston *Independent Chronicle* in March 1807:

> President JEFFERSON
>
> This day published, price 1 dollar — a Print of THOMAS JEFFERSON — engraved by ROBERT FIELD, from a Picture by GILBERT STUART,
>
> To be had at the Publishers in Devonshire-street, and at the various Booksellers.[3]

Field, who had painted Jefferson in watercolor about 1798,[4] produced an exceptionally fine print (fig. 38). His biographer has described it as "Field's best plate and an unusually beautiful example of the dotted style," accurately reproducing "every detail and

[1] Jefferson to Henry Dearborn, July 5, 1819, Andrew A. Lipscomb and Albert E. Bergh, eds., *The Writings of Thomas Jefferson*, 20 vols. (Washington, D.C., 1903), 19: 271.

[2] See pp. 31–41 above.

[3] *Independent Chronicle*, Mar. 23, 30, 1807.

[4] Bush, "Life Portraits of Jefferson," pp. 48–50.

Fig. 38. Thomas Jefferson. Engraving by Robert Field, Boston, March 14, 1807

the colour values of the original."[5] The engraving is signed "G. Stuart. Pinxit" and "R. Field. Sculpsit." It is dated "Boston, Published by Robert Field, March 14th 1807." Whatever may be said of other engravings offered to the public, in this instance the ordinary person could purchase for a dollar an accurate, beautifully executed engraving of a recent portrait of the president by the country's most famous portrait painter.

The engraving was taken from the Jefferson portrait that Stuart painted for James Bowdoin III (Appendix, plate VI) soon after he persuaded Jefferson to sit for a second time. Although there is no question that the painting for Bowdoin derives from the second sitting, there has been much debate as to which of the three portraits that came from that same sitting was the original one drawn from life. Was it the portrait that Jefferson, after being put off by Stuart for years, finally received from the artist in 1821 (the "Edgehill" portrait), or the example that Stuart painted for Madison, or the canvas that Bowdoin received?

The leading authorities agree that the "Edgehill" portrait is the original likeness taken from life.[6] Jefferson referred to the portrait in Madison's possession as a copy, writing, while Madison was president, that he had "no doubt that the copy of my portrait at the President's residence in Orange . . . is as good as the original in the possession of Stewart."[7] That Madison's replica was completed be-

[5] Harry Piers, *Robert Field: Portrait Painter in Oils, Miniature, and Water-Colours and Engraver* (New York, 1927), p. 195.

[6] Kimball, "Life Portraits of Jefferson," pp. 516–20; Bush, "Life Portraits of Jefferson," pp. 73–74; Sadik, *Colonial and Federal Portraits*, pp. 159–61.

[7] Jefferson to Joseph Delaplaine, May 20, 1816, Jefferson Papers, Lib. Cong. See also Jefferson to Delaplaine, May 3, 1814, Lipscomb and Bergh, eds., *Jefferson Writings*, 14: 134. The portrait owned by Madison is now owned by Colonial Williamsburg and hangs in the reconstructed colonial Virginia Capitol.

fore the work for Bowdoin is established by the evidence that William Dunlap saw Madison's painting early in 1806;[8] it seems likely that Stuart finished it before he left Washington for Boston in July 1805. There is no record that Jefferson was aware of the painting for Bowdoin, although his secretary of war, Henry Dearborn, arranged for Stuart to accept Bowdoin's commission for the work. Dearborn reported in late June 1805 that Stuart had nearly completed the portrait for Bowdoin and would take the incompleted canvas with him when he left Washington.[9] Stuart finished the portrait for Bowdoin in Boston, probably in 1807.[10]

Field's use of a column that appears in the background in the Bowdoin *Jefferson* but not in Madison's replica or the "Edgehill" portrait indicates that he took his engraving from the Bowdoin painting. This is, however, of only incidental interest, for the head of Jefferson in all three paintings is nearly identical. In view of Stuart's habit of delay in regard to engravings, the appearance of Field's print within two years after the painting of the original likeness was an extraordinary accomplishment, the significance of which is more apparent to historians than it was to the readers who saw the small notice announcing Field's print in the Boston papers of 1807.

Although Stuart's excuse for retaining Jefferson's portrait in his possession was his wish to have an engraving made from it, Jefferson got no portrait even after Field's print appeared. In 1814 he wrote to Stuart on the matter, explaining: "You wished to retain the portrait which you were so kind to make of me while in Washing-

[8] See p. 1, n. 2 above.

[9] Sadik, *Colonial and Federal Portraits*, pp. 155, 156, 159; Dearborn to Thomas L. Winthrop, June 27, 1805, quoted in Kimball, "Life Portraits of Jefferson," p. 518.

[10] See Kimball, "Life Portraits of Jefferson," pp. 518–20; Sadik, *Colonial and Federal Portraits*, pp. 160–61. The Bowdoin painting is now in the Bowdoin College Museum of Art.

ton, until you should have time to have a print copied from it. This, I believe has been done, at least I think I have seen one which appeared to have been taken from that portrait."[11] Although this letter was written seven years after Field's print appeared, it drew no response from Stuart; indeed, another seven years would pass before Jefferson received his portrait from the artist. Jefferson's letter is of particular interest here in showing that he was familiar with Field's print.

Field's engraving was copied almost immediately after it appeared. The Stuart image of Jefferson that could have come only from that print appeared on a political broadside published in New York in June 1807 (see fig. 52). Although images of political figures were rarely seen on the political broadsides of the time, the unusual print is dominated by two carefully engraved portraits of Washington and Jefferson. Neither the artist nor the circumstance that produced the print is known. Because the print, despite the accuracy of the portraits, was presented as a caricature, it has been so treated in this work and will be more fully described below.[12]

As Jefferson later recalled, it was soon after he sat for Stuart for a second time that he got Stuart to sketch him "in the medallion form."[13] His account books show that he paid Stuart one hundred dollars for this on June 7, 1805, and on June 18 he wrote to Stuart:

> Mr. Jefferson presents his compliments to Mr. Stewart, and begs leave to send him the enclosed for the trouble he gave him in taking the head à la antique. Mr. Stewart seemed to contemplate having an engraving made either from that or the first portrait; he is free to use

[11] Jefferson to Stuart, Aug. 9, 1814, quoted in Kimball, "Life Portraits of Jefferson," p. 512.

[12] See p. 115 below.

[13] Jefferson to Henry Dearborn, July 5, 1819, Lipscomb and Bergh, eds., *Jefferson Writings*, 19: 271.

> either the one or the other at his choice; the one not proposed to be used I will be glad to receive at Mr. Stewart's convenience; the other when he shall be done with it.[14]

Stuart chose to retain the larger oil portrait and sent Jefferson the medallion profile, which Jefferson regarded as fragile but very fine.[15]

The profile (Appendix, plate VII) was hung in the President's House, where William Birch admired it about October 1805 and received Jefferson's permission to borrow it for two days to make a drawing of it. It was Birch's copy that was used by David Edwin in making his superb engraving in 1809 (fig. 39).[16] In sending Jefferson some impressions from that plate and thanking him again for the use of the original, Birch wrote:

> You at that time expressed your approbation of my wish to engrave it, when I found Mr. Stuart had no intentions to publish it himself, I got Mr. Edwin to engrave it for me, as being Superior in that line to myself; I think it forms a b[ea]utiful imitation of the Antiqua, and a strong likeness of yourself.

Birch also went on to say that he had the plate engraved "for no other purpose than that a proper Likeness of you may be circulated," and that "my purpose is to give them away."[17] The plate is inscribed "G. Stuart Pinx W. Birch delin. D. Edwin sc. 1809. Copy Right Secured according to Law."

[14]Jefferson to Stuart, June 18, 1805, quoted in Kimball, "Life Portraits of Jefferson," p. 512.

[15]Jefferson to Henry Dearborn, July 5, 1819, Lipscomb and Bergh, eds., *Jefferson Writings*, 19: 271. The medallion portrait is now in the Fogg Art Museum, Harvard University.

[16]Bush, "Life Portraits of Jefferson," p. 79.

[17]William Birch to Jefferson, July 8, 1812, Jefferson Papers, Lib. Cong.

Fig. 39. Thomas Jefferson. Engraving by David Edwin, 1809

Jefferson was clearly pleased with the engraving, writing to Birch that the prints were "an elegant specimen of Mr. Edwin's talent in this line, and prove also that the design has well conformed to the original." Later, when he presented one of the prints to a friend, he described it as "a profile, engraved by Edwin, from an original drawn by Stewart, and deemed the best which has been taken of me."[18] Unfortunately, the number of Jefferson's contemporaries who got to see the print was not large. It is not known how many copies Birch gave away, but the plate was ruined in an effort to rebite it after only a few impressions were made.[19] Although never widely distributed among his contemporaries, the likeness would later be copied and become one of the most enduring of Jefferson's images.

[18] Jefferson to Birch, Aug. 3, 1812, ibid.; Jefferson to Horatio G. Spafford, Feb. 21, 1815, Jefferson Papers, Coolidge Collection, Mass. Hist. Soc., microfilm edition.

[19] Bush, "Life Portraits of Jefferson," p. 16.

CHAPTER VIII

Household Images

IN THE LATE EIGHTEENTH AND EARLY NINETEENTH centuries the flourishing pottery industry in Liverpool, England, produced a variety of pieces decorated with scenic views, ships, portraits, and even caricatures. For the American market — a major buyer of the cream-colored earthenware — there were numerous pitchers, mugs, and other pieces adorned with American ships and American heroes. The simple decorative technique consisted of making a print on paper from an ordinary engraved copperplate and, while the ink was wet, transferring the print by pressure to the glazed pottery and then fixing the impression by firing. Thus, many engravings that appeared in prints also were used on Liverpool ware. Washington's portrait was a popular image on Liverpool pieces made for America, and his death in 1799 produced a large number of commemorative designs.[1]

After the inauguration of Jefferson as president, English pottery makers rushed to supply American customers with ware adorned with the image of their new leader. Unfortunately, the

[1] Robert H. McCauley, *Liverpool Transfer Designs on Anglo-American Pottery* (Portland, Me., 1942), pp. 7, 15–16; Alan Smith, *The Illustrated Guide to Liverpool Herculaneum Pottery, 1796–1840* (New York, 1970), pp. 57–58.

availability of a likeness of the new president was limited. Nevertheless, pottery designers, who rarely gave much attention to the quality of proper likenesses, proceeded to supply the anticipated demand. One piece displaying a figure purporting to be Jefferson (fig. 40) bears no resemblance whatever to any portrait, image, or engraving of Jefferson. It is clearly someone else and was probably produced before any of the prints of Jefferson reached England.[2] The most readily available print of Jefferson in England shortly after his inauguration was the inaccurate drawing engraved by Edward Orme, published in London in August 1801 and reprinted in the widely circulating *European Magazine, and London Review* in May 1802.[3] It was that distorted image of the Orme print and its derivatives, such as that engraved by Friedrich Wilhelm Nettling in Leipzig, which was seized upon by the pottery makers, and it is the image most often found today on surviving pieces of Liverpool ware.

Five different pieces of Liverpool pottery with this image have been located — four pitchers and one mug (figs. 41–45). Each piece is distinct, but all have the same portrait. Two of the pitchers are decorated on one side with pictures of ships and two, with verses. One pitcher also is adorned under the spout with an excerpt from Jefferson's first inaugural address — "Peace, Commerce and honest Friendship with all Nations, Entangling Alliances with none" — beneath a representation of the Seal of the United States. It is dated 1802 (fig. 42). On all pieces the portraits are clearly identified as "Thomas Jefferson, President of the United States of America." On three of the pitchers the portraits are embellished with garlands containing the names of the states. Since only fifteen states, instead of the sixteen in the Union at the time of Jefferson's election, are named, these designs may well have previously framed an earlier American patriot.

[2]The opposite side of the pitcher has a profile portrait of Washington with the words: "He in Glory, America in Tears," suggesting its appearance soon after Washington's death in December 1799 (National Museum of History and Technology, Smithsonian Institution).

[3]See pp. 40–43 above.

Fig. 40. Unknown figure identified as Jefferson on Liverpool pitcher, ca. 1800

Fig. 41. Jefferson portrait on Liverpool pitcher, ca. 1801

Fig. 42. Jefferson portrait on Liverpool pitcher, 1802

Fig. 43. Jefferson portrait on Liverpool pitcher, ca. 1801

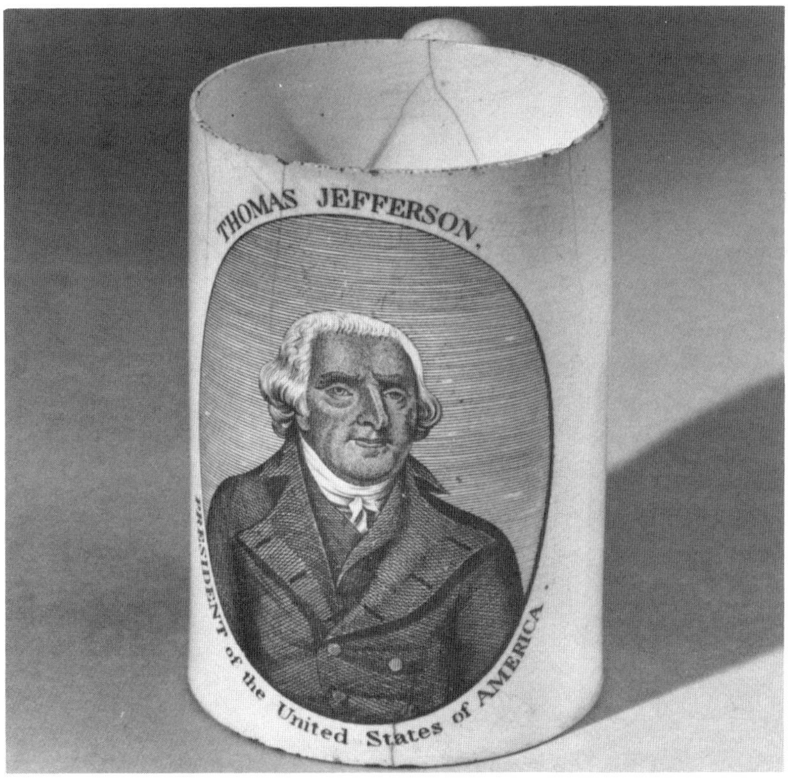

Fig. 44. Jefferson portrait on Liverpool mug, ca. 1801

Fig. 45. Jefferson portrait on Liverpool pitcher, ca. 1801

Besides using outdated designs, some pottery makers substituted new names to identify old portraits, as they did for Jefferson in the example cited earlier (see fig. 40). A portrait of Jefferson (fig. 45) also was used at least once as a portrait of President Madison, the only change being in the banner, which was altered to read "James Maddison, President of the United States of America" (fig. 46).[4] Perhaps the most unusual example of a potter's resourceful use of his stock of engravings is the example of a hatted, sullen-looking figure that appeared as both President Jefferson (fig. 47) and President Monroe (fig. 48) and represented neither.[5]

[4]The potters not only fooled contemporaries, they have also misled at least one recent writer, who described the portrait as copied from a painting of Madison by John Vanderlyn and noted that "the engraving is quite close in appearance to the original" (Mariam Klamkin, *American Patriotic and Political China* [New York 1973], p. 77).

[5]McCauley reproduced the Monroe example and found the same portrait identified as Phillip Crandall and I. Baker on two other Liverpool pitchers. He was unaware of the Jefferson example (McCauley, *Liverpool Transfer Designs*, pp. 43, 80).

Fig. 46. Jefferson portrait identified as James Madison on Liverpool pitcher, ca. 1810

When a portrait was used to decorate a piece, it usually dominated the design, but one pottery maker presented a small likeness of Jefferson framed by two doves (fig. 49) above a verse which proclaimed:

Hail Columbia happy land
Hail ye patriotic band
Who late oppos'd oppressive laws
And now stand firm in freedom's cause
Rejoice for now the storm is gone
Columbia owns her chosen son
The rights of man shall be our boast
And jefferson our fav'rite toast
Republicans behold your chief
He comes to give your fears relief
Now arm'd in virtue firm and true
Looks for support to Heaven and you[6]

The verse, even more than the portrait, shows that such pieces were produced exclusively for the American market.

[6] Pitcher, [ca. 1801], National Museum of History and Technology, Smithsonian Institution.

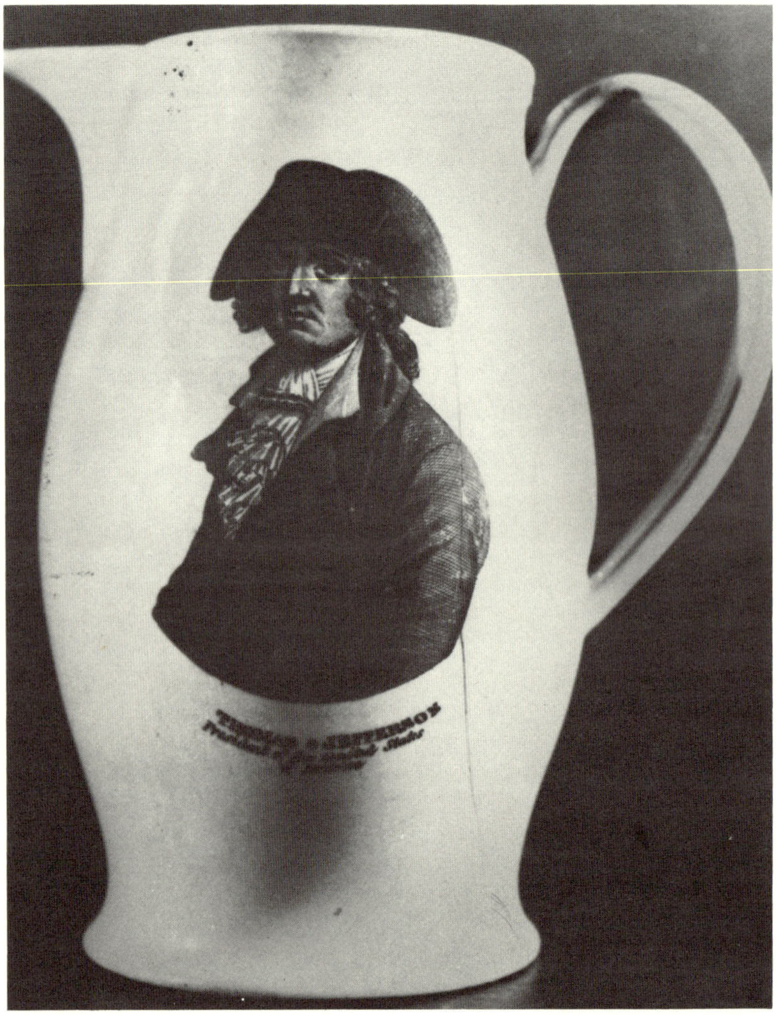

Fig. 47. Unknown figure identified as Jefferson on Liverpool pitcher

The use of caricatures as transfers on Liverpool pottery was not extensive, but one cartoon that includes a figure labeled Jefferson (fig. 50) appeared in at least two versions on Liverpool pieces.[7]

[7]One version of the print is shown in fig. 50; another version is illustrated in Willard E. Keyes, "The Cow and the Sleeping Lion," *Antiques* 39 (1941): 27. The latter example has been credited to James Akin by Nina Fletcher Little in "The Cartoons of James Akin upon Liverpool Ware," *Bulletin of the Society for the Preservation of New England Antiquities* 28 (1938): 106–8; but no print of the caricature is known, and Akin's authorship has not been documented.

Fig. 48. Unknown figure identified as James Monroe on Liverpool pitcher

Occupying the center of the scene, however, is not Jefferson but a cow, representing American commerce. The horns of the cow are being held by John Bull and the tail pulled by Napoleon. A seated figure wearing a large hat is milking the cow and would be unrecognizable were he not labeled "Jefferson." If the meaning is not entirely clear, it is because the drawing was adapted from a frequently copied cow caricature of the period of the American Revolution in which the cow represented British commerce. Originally

Fig. 49. Liverpool pitcher, ca. 1801

Fig. 50. Liverpool pitcher, ca. 1808–9

Fig. 51. Jefferson portrait on Liverpool pitcher, 1801

engraved in England, the cow caricature also appeared in French and Dutch versions during the Revolutionary era.[8] The print in which "Jefferson" appeared, therefore, belongs less in a study of Jefferson caricature than in a study of the cow in caricature, and it has little significance as a portrayal of the popular image of Jefferson.

The most pleasing portrait of Jefferson discovered on a piece of Liverpool pottery offers a likeness that derived from Rembrandt Peale's 1800 painting, although an engraved print of this particular derivative has not been found. The pitcher displaying this portrait is elaborately decorated, Jefferson's picture being framed by a wreath with stars and the names of the states. Above is a motto from Jefferson's first inaugural address: "We are all Republicans — all Federalists." Below, the portrait is inscribed "Thomas Jefferson President of the United States of America 1801" (fig. 51).

If surviving examples are indicative, this likeness was seen far less often than the image from the Edward Orme print, which wide circulation not only made available but also gave authenticity. The reader who opened the *European Magazine* for May 1802 and saw the portrait of Jefferson attributed to Gilbert Stuart[9] would not have been surprised when he saw the same print on a Liverpool pitcher or mug. If he bought the piece, he probably felt reassured that he was getting an authentic portrait. For Americans who never read the *European Magazine*, the pieces of Liverpool pottery that found their way into their homes may have been the only source of their visual image of President Jefferson.

[8] An examination of the origins and popularity of the cow in caricature can be found in Keyes, "The Cow and the Sleeping Lion," *Antiques* 39 (1941): 25–27.

[9] See pp. 42–45 above.

CHAPTER IX

Jefferson in Caricature

THE FREQUENT REPRODUCTION OF CARICATURES contemporary with Jefferson's presidency in works of history may have contributed to a misleading impression that such caricatures circulated widely in Jefferson's day. The fact is that they did not. Cartoons almost never appeared in newspapers,[1] and only rarely were they published in books or magazines. Most of the caricatures that were published were sold as individual prints, often hand-colored. While newspaper advertisements and publishers' records show that engraved portraits had a wide market throughout the United States, hardly a reference can be found to caricatures. It would be a mistake to assume that many of Jefferson's contemporaries ever

[1]The earliest newspaper found to contain editorial caricatures is the Poughkeepsie, New York, *Farmers' and Mechanics' Repository*, of which the only known issues are nos. 1 and 2 of vol. 1, published in Dec. 1809. The caricature published in the second number (Dec. 9, 1809) is reproduced in American Antiquarian Society, *Reports for the Year 1978*, opposite p. 138; see also pp. 144–45. William Murrell, *A History of American Graphic Humor*, 2 vols. (New York, 1933–38), 1: 74–76, cited a cartoon published in the *New-York Evening Post* in 1814 as the first cartoon designed for newspaper reproduction in the United States.

saw a caricature of him. Had such prints enjoyed a wide distribution, it might be expected that mention of them would be found in contemporary letters or diaries; but if such references exist, none has been located. If Jefferson was familiar with caricatures in which he appeared, it is not evident from his own papers.

The number of prints depicting Jefferson in caricature is not large, and in some of them the resemblance to him is so poor as to raise the question whether the artist had any clear image of Jefferson's physical features in his own mind. In a few important instances the image of Jefferson shows its derivation from one of the engraved portrait prints.

Before his election to the presidency, Jefferson was depicted in recognizable form in at least two political caricatures. One print, published during Washington's presidency, shows Jefferson along with James Madison and Albert Gallatin trying to stop the wheels of government, represented by Washington in his carriage leading an army of marching volunteers.[2] Another well-executed print portrays a kneeling Jefferson about to sacrifice the Constitution on the "altar to Gallic despotism" when an American eagle rescues the document from the flames.[3] Jefferson may have been included in

[2]"The Times; a Political Portrait," undated print in New-York Historical Society; reproduced in Thomas C. Blaisdell, Jr., Peter Selz, et al., *The American Presidency in Political Cartoons: 1776–1976* (Berkeley, Calif., 1976), p. 41, and Murrell, *American Graphic Humor*, 1: 36. The caption reads: "Triumph Government: perish all its enemies. — Traitors be warned: justice though slow, is sure." The identity of some of the figures in this print is open to question. Murrell (1: 38) identified Jefferson's accomplices as Gallatin and Edmond Charles Genet rather than Madison and Gallatin.

[3]"The Providential Detection," undated print in Library Company of Philadelphia and American Antiquarian Society; reproduced in Blaisdell, *The American Presidency in Political Cartoons*, p. 43. This print was tentatively dated 1800 in Frank Weitenkampf, *Political Caricature in the United States in Separately Published Cartoons* (New York, 1953), p. 13, but the prints at both the Library Com-

other caricatures in the 1790s, but the crudely drawn figures in some cartoons are not always identifiable today and may even have not been recognized by contemporaries.[4]

Not a single cartoon has been found that can be authoritatively identified as a product of the presidential campaign of 1800 — a finding that strikingly demonstrates the undeveloped state of political caricature in the United States at the time of Jefferson's election. Political pamphlets, handbills, and newspapers were all extensively employed during that campaign, but none of them contained either portraits or caricatures. The same circumstances persisted after Jefferson took office. If Jefferson was portrayed in any published caricature during his first term as president, no example has been located.[5] The earliest known example from Jefferson's

---

pany of Philadelphia and the American Antiquarian Society are watermarked 1794, and a date about 1797 has been suggested by Gordon N. Marshall of the Library Company of Philadelphia (see *Made in America, Printmaking 1760–1860: An Exhibition of Original Prints from the Collections of the Library Company of Philadelphia and the Historical Society of Pennsylvania, April-June, 1973* [Philadelphia, 1973], pp. 13–14).

[4] One of the figures in a caricature entitled "A Peep into the Antifederalist Club," published in New York, Aug. 16, 1793, has elsewhere been identified as Jefferson, but the figure could as easily be Aaron Burr. The print is reproduced and described in *Made in America, Print-making 1760–1860*, pp. 11–12. A print entitled "Mad Tom in a Rage" has often been mistakenly identified as representing Jefferson, although it was correctly identified as being Thomas Paine in Weitenkampf, *Political Caricature in the United States*, p. 13.

[5] There is a crude drawing entitled "Presidential-Bull-Bait," dated Feb. 4, 1805, relating to attempts to gain West Florida, in the New York Public Library. The drawing shows an unrecognizable figure representing Jefferson encouraging congressional dogs (labeled with names of congressmen) against a bull representing Spain. No evidence has been found that this drawing was ever engraved. The drawing is reproduced in Stefan Lorant, *The Glorious Burden: The American Presidency* (New York, 1968), p. 73.

Fig. 52. Political caricature, New York, June 1807. By unknown artist

presidential years is a print engraved by James Akin entitled "The Prairie Dog Sickened at the sting of the Hornet," which shows a dog with a head representing Jefferson being stung by a hornet representing Napoleon. The dog is coughing up coins into a pile labeled "Two Millions!" The print is not dated, but the allusion to the Two-Million Dollar Act places it in 1806.[6] Akin was living in Newburyport, Massachusetts, at the time this political print was published, and it is questionable whether many people outside Newburyport ever saw it.

[6] Akin was advertising himself as the author of the print in Nov. 1806. The print is reproduced and described in Maureen O'Brien Quimby, "The Political Art of James Akin," *Winterthur Portfolio 7* (Charlottesville, Va., 1972), pp. 64, 66–68, 96. Quimby's dating of the print as 1803–4 cannot be accepted.

Jefferson was midway through his second term when the first important presidential caricature appeared in New York in June 1807 (fig. 52). This political broadside from an exceptionally well-executed plate is a caricature only in the setting in which accurately engraved portraits of Washington and Jefferson taken from Gilbert Stuart are displayed. Washington is shown beneath a halolike wreath with rays extending from it, and his portrait rests on three books inscribed Order, Law, and Religion. Jefferson's portrait rests on books inscribed Sophisms, Notes on Virginia, Tom Paine, Condorcet, and Voltaire; and above his head a burning candle produces a darkening cloud. A stately lion and an American eagle flank Washington's portrait. Beneath Jefferson's picture a coiled snake and a lizard provide the contrast. Viewers are asked to "LOOK ON THIS PICTURE, AND ON THIS" — a line from a passage in *Hamlet* that is continued under the two pictures. Shakespeare's verse heaps praise upon Washington and presents Jefferson "like a mildew'd ear, Blasting his wholesome brother."[7] The picture of Jefferson was taken from the engraving by Robert Field of Stuart's 1805 portrait of Jefferson.[8]

The embargo enacted in December 1807 in response to the British attack on the *Chesapeake* produced the greatest popular discontent with Jefferson's administration of any policy of his eight years in office, and it was the one issue of his presidency that most prompted artistic satirists to take up their pens. There are no less than five important caricatures that were inspired by the embargo,

[7] Under Washington were the lines:

> See what a grace was seated on this brow:
> An eye like Mars to threaten and command,
> A combination and a form, indeed,
> Where every God did seem to set his seal,
> To give the world assurance of a man.

The words are all Shakespeare's, but some lines were omitted from the passage quoted, which is found in *Hamlet*, Act III, Scene IV.

[8] There are copies of the print in both the New-York Historical Society and the New York Public Library.

Fig. 53. English political caricature by Cruikshank, 1808

at least one of which was published in England. The English example (fig. 53) is signed by Cruikshank, dated October 1, 1808, and titled "The happy Effects of that Grand Systom of shutting Ports against the English!!" The print pictures Jefferson standing on a dais addressing a group of disgruntled citizens on his "Grand Philosophical Idea — shutting our Ports against the English." He is saying that "if we continue the Experiment for about fifteen or twenty years, we may begin then to feel the good *Effects* — in the mean time to prevent our sailors from being idle, I would advise you to imploy them in various works of husbandry &c." Although drawn by one of England's most celebrated caricaturists, the figure

Fig. 54. Political cartoon by unknown artist, ca. 1808–9

of Jefferson does not appear to have been modeled after any known likeness and simply represents a presidential-looking figure.[9]

[9]The print is described in Mary Dorothy George, *Catalogue of Political and Personal Satires Preserved in the Department of Prints and Drawings of the British Museum*, 8 (London, 1947): 681. George lists the print as by Isaac and/or George Cruikshank, "Pubd. Walker 7 Cornhill Octr. 1, 1808." See also M. Dorothy George, *English Political Caricature, 1793–1832* (Oxford, 1959), p. 115. This is the only English caricature depicting Jefferson listed by George. One of the original colored prints hangs in the library at Monticello.

A print entitled "King Quilldriver's Experiments on National Defence," dated 1808, is much in the style of English caricature, such as that of Isaac Cruikshank,[10] but it is signed "Peter Pencil," an unknown artist whose work has been accepted as American.[11] It depicts Jefferson in a huge Napoleonic hat holding a quill-pen sword in one hand and the embargo proclamation in the other, standing within a fortress of proclamations.[12] Though the central figure is unmistakably a representation of Jefferson, the artist does not appear to have attempted a likeness or copied an engraving. Jefferson is hardly more recognizable in a three-frame cartoon sketch of the embargo act, which shows Jefferson and Madison hauling a ship into dry dock at the command of Napoleon, while behind a curtain a dissatisfied Congress debates the embargo (fig. 54).[13] Though undated, the subject matter indicates that it was drawn in 1808 or early 1809.

The best caricatures relating to the period of the embargo and the most successful in depicting Jefferson of any that appeared during his presidency are two prints produced by the unidentified "Peter Pencil," a skillful engraver whose real identity would be of great interest. Both prints are signed and dated 1809, though,

[10]See E. B. Krumbhaar, *Isaac Cruikshank: A Catalogue Raisonné with a Sketch of His Life and Work* (Philadelphia, 1966), plates 86, 205, 380.

[11]Murrell, *American Graphic Humor*, 1: 64.

[12]The print is reproduced in Roger Butterfield, *The American Past* (New York, 1966), p. 49, and in Murrell, *American Graphic Humor*, 1: 56.

[13]The print is unsigned, undated, and untitled, though on the only copy known there is written in ink above the frame showing Jefferson: "An old Philosopher teaching his mad Son economical Projects" (Free Library of Philadelphia). The print is reproduced and described in Blaisdell, *The American Presidency in Political Cartoons*, pp. 50–51; it is also described in detail in Weitenkampf, *Political Caricature in the United States*, pp. 15–16.

curiously, one is signed "Peter Pencil" and the other, "Peter Pencill." The fine copperplate impressions are similar in style, composition, and size and are printed in sepia ink on the same type of paper — an unusually heavy variety for this kind of caricature. The only known copies of the prints, in the Houghton Library at Harvard, are in exceptionally good condition and clearly were never passed from hand to hand by Jefferson's contemporaries. Who produced the prints or where they were displayed is unknown. No contemporary reference to either print or to "Peter Pencil" has been located. The prints were obviously designed as a pair, and the head of Jefferson in each is similar and is copied from David Edwin's engraving after Rembrandt Peale. Whoever "Peter Pencil" was, he had access to that influential engraving copied by so many other engravers after its publication in 1800. Most of the work on the two plates was done by etching, but the heads of all figures were done in stipple. The print entitled "Intercourse or Impartial Dealings" (fig. 55) shows Jefferson submitting to a club-wielding George III, while Napoleon empties his pockets.[14] The print entitled "Non Intercourse or Dignified Retirement" (fig. 56) shows Jefferson in shirt sleeves and ragged breeches with his coat on the ground. He is saying: "What a fine thing it is to feel Independent of all Taylors! I have stript myself rather than submit to London or Parisian Fashion! — Dear me! how unwise it would be ever more

[14] George III says: "Well Tommy! I brought you at last to close Quarters therefore mind what you are about! — If you dont behave gently I'll break your limbs and leave you the rest. let me tell you my Boy, keep yourself Cool!"

Jefferson replies: "Cool? Aye! to be sure! I always keep myself Cool when I get into a Passion; but I must say Lord! have mercy upon us! what an Enormity! to pull my coat on the Highway of all Nations! Lord! what an Inconvenient Restriction."

Napoleon says: "Trés bien! Mon Oncle Thomas! Dat is very vell! de more you make one Noise, de less dat Jean Boule vill see, dat ve are And and Gloves. N'oubliez pas dat I am de And — I want de money and must ave it!" Houghton Library, Harvard.

Fig. 55. *"Intercourse or Impartial Dealings," by "Peter Pencil," 1809*

Fig. 56. "*Non Intercourse or Dignified Retirement,*" *by* "*Peter Pencill,*" *1809*

to recur to the London Cut! it never Suited me. — they are always wrong in their Measures." To the side, Napoleon applauds and says that Jefferson now has only to take off his shirt of Irish linen.[15]

How many of Jefferson's contemporaries may have seen these prints or any of the other caricatures of Jefferson as president cannot be known, but there is no reason to think that it was a large number. Those who may have seen the pair of "Peter Pencil" engravings would have seen a likeness of Jefferson that must have been familiar to them by 1809, and those prints confirm again the importance of Edwin's 1800 engraving of Rembrandt Peale's first portrait of Jefferson. Yet despite these interesting examples of Jefferson in caricature, cartoons were not very important in the circulation of Jefferson's image among his contemporaries.[16]

[15] Napoleon's words are: "Bravissimo! mon Oncle Thomas! I give you — maparole d'honneur, séconde qualité, dat I am very much content of you — you ave only to take off de Chémise car c'est de la Toile d'Irelande and you will ave donné one grand example of one Sacrifice généreux." Houghton Library, Harvard.

[16] Omitted from the above examination of Jefferson in caricature is the following work: *Hugginiana; or Huggins' Fantasy, Being a Collection of the Most Esteemed Modern Literary Productions . . . by John Richard Desborus Huggins* (4th ed., New York: Printed by H. C. Southwick, No. 2, Wall-Street, Most Excellent Printer to his most Barber-ous Majesty, 1808). Huggins was a barber who wrote humorous advertisements, and these were collected by him in the above volume. Included in the work was a series of engravings signed "Tisdale Delt. Leney Scul." Figures designated as Jefferson appear in several plates in this series, but none bears any resemblance to Jefferson. This is an unusual personal publication about which there is inadequate information, and the prints cannot be accepted as significant in relation to Jefferson in caricature. The work is described in Murrell, *American Graphic Humor*, 1: 55–60, where it is viewed as an important work in American cartoons.

CHAPTER X

Silhouettes

SILHOUETTES WERE ONE MEANS FOR THE POPULAR dissemination of Jefferson's image, but the number of different silhouettes made and the extent of their distribution is impossible to establish with any certainty, for the nature of the inexpensive paper profiles did not promote their preservation. In June 1803 Uri H. Hill called on President Jefferson with a note from inventor John I. Hawkins stating: "I take the liberty to request as a favor you will permit the bearer Mr. Uri H. Hill to take your likeness in Profile with one of my Patent Physiognatraces, and would also ask leave to Publish copies of the same, here and in Europe." Jefferson had earlier been "struck with notice in the papers of Mr. Hawkins's physiognotrace" and had asked Charles Willson Peale, to whose Philadelphia museum Hawkins had given one of his devices, for "an explanation of the principle of it." Peale had supplied both a detailed explanation and a drawing.[1] Under these circumstances, it may be assumed that the president would have been eager to have a demonstration of the mechanism and that he permitted Hill to

[1] Hawkins to Jefferson, June 8, 1803, received June 14, 1803, Jefferson Papers, Coolidge Collection, Mass. Hist. Soc., microfilm edition; Jefferson to Peale, Jan. 23, 1803, Peale to Jefferson, Jan. 28, 1803, Jefferson Papers, Lib. Cong.

take his profile; also, it would have been uncharacteristic of Jefferson not to have granted his permission for copies to be published. Yet, if copies of this profile have survived, none has been recognized, and no other contemporary record of it has been found.

There are, however, two silhouettes of Jefferson that can be documented as having been available to the public during his presidency. The earliest of these was taken from Houdon's bust (Appendix, plate I) by means of Hawkins's physiognotrace. With Hawkins's device a brass rod with a thin edge was run lightly around the subject's head, and by means of a pantograph the form of the profile was traced onto paper, producing, according to Charles Willson Peale, in "a diminished size a perfectly correct representation." With a twice-folded piece of paper, four identical silhouettes could be scissored from one tracing.[2] After installing Hawkins's invention in his museum, Peale in January 1803 sent Jefferson some of the profiles he had made from Houdon's bust. Peale also gave away these silhouettes at the museum. "Several hundreds taken from Houdons Bust I have dispersed," he told Jefferson in 1804, "altho' I kept them out of sight, and meant to be a favor." But though several hundreds were given away, none is known to have survived today.[3]

The size of this profile was not good for framing, Peale thought, and in 1804 he and his son Raphaelle took steps to make a new silhouette of Jefferson, taken from life. Peale appealed to Jefferson for assistance in the enterprise, writing from Baltimore in June 1804:

> My Sons here are very desireous of having the outline of your profile taken in the size which the Argand Lamp will give on the wall, resting the head against a beer or other long Glass. It will only

[2] Peale, "Explanation of Mr. John I. Hawkins Physiognotrace," Peale to Jefferson, Jan. 28, 1803, Jefferson Papers, Lib. Cong.; Sellers, *Charles Willson Peale*, 2: 158.

[3] Peale to Jefferson, Jan. 10, 1803, June 15, 1804, Jefferson to Peale, Jan. 23, 1803, Jefferson Papers, Lib. Cong.

> be a loss of one minute of time to sit while Mr. Burrell might trace the shadow with a Pencil, from which my Son Raphaelle can cut it out, and with his Physiognotrace produce numbers. The Profiles I have generally seen of you are not so critically like as I would wish them. But the best apology I can make for asking this favour, is, that my Sons desire to present them to every visitor of the Exhibition of the Skeleton, which will be a gratification to your numerous friends.[4]

Jefferson obliged his friend and had his private secretary, William A. Burwell, make two drawings of his profile, which he sent to Peale.[5] Burwell's skills at drawing, however, left much to be desired, and Charles Willson Peale's disappointment was evident as he wrote to Raphaelle and Rembrandt: "I have just received two attempts at the profiles of Mr. Jefferson by Mr. Burrell, they are so miserably done that I have had my doubts whether I ought to send them, however with a profile taken from Houdons bust, which I send, you may perhaps make something of a likeness, but whether of sufficient accuracy to do you credit I cannot say." Apparently Raphaelle and Rembrandt were no happier with Burwell's efforts than their father was, and Raphaelle decided to go to Washington to take Jefferson's profile himself. A month later the elder Peale was writing Jefferson: "We are much pleased with the profiles done by my Son Raphaelle. I wish he had also taken some of Mr. Madison and Mr. Gallitine — but he had no other object then, for his journey to Washington."[6]

Although it cannot be claimed with certainty, it may be that it was this profile by Raphaelle Peale to which Henry Dearborn referred when he wrote to Jefferson in August 1804: "Please to accept my thanks for the profile you were good enough to enclose, it

[4] Peale to Jefferson, June 15, 1804, ibid.

[5] Jefferson to Peale, June 20, 1804, ibid.

[6] Charles Willson Peale to Raphaelle and Rembrandt Peale, June 23, 1804, Charles Willson Peale letter book, Am. Phil. Soc.; Charles Willson Peale to Jefferson, July 24, 1804, Jefferson Papers, Lib. Cong.

Fig. 57. Silhouette of Jefferson by Raphaelle Peale, 1804

strikes me as the only good likeness, except Stuarts, I have ever seen of the original, which very much enhances its value."[7] This may seem extravagant praise for a silhouette, but it might also reflect Dearborn's dissatisfaction with the various engravings pub-

[7] Dearborn to Jefferson, Aug. 23, 1804, Jefferson Papers, Lib. Cong.

lished during the first years of Jefferson's presidency and his preference for a good profile over a poor portrait. There is also no other known profile that so well fits the available evidence.[8]

One of the silhouettes made by Raphaelle Peale is now at Monticello (fig. 57). The profile was cut from white paper 4½ by 3⅞ inches, which, when placed over black, produced a shadow portrait 2⅞ by 1¾ inches. Immediately below the profile "PEALE" is embossed in a curved rectangle.[9] Raphaelle Peale made his silhouettes using a portable physiognotrace developed from Hawkins's invention and advertised his work as a "Facietrace." He traveled through the country charging twenty-five cents for cutting a profile; he also offered frames for sale at twenty-five cents with "a silhouette of Washington, Adams, or Jefferson, your choice, thrown in."[10] Thus, as in the case of the silhouette from Houdon's bust, silhouettes of Jefferson were given away — a circumstance that may have contributed to a lack of concern for their preservation and thus to the rarity of Peale's silhouette today. Charles Willson Peale regarded

[8]The profile by Saint-Mémin was not made until Nov. 1804 (see pp. 81–82 above). The profile on glass by Doolittle (see p. 135 below) had been completed by the time of Dearborn's letter, but it seems unlikely that, with opportunities to present Dearborn with that profile when both men were in Washington, Jefferson would choose to mail the fragile profile to Dearborn while both men were on vacation — Jefferson at Monticello and Dearborn in Maine. It also seems unlikely that Dearborn would refer to a glass profile as enclosed in a letter.

[9]This was the mark used by Raphaelle Peale; silhouettes made at Peale's Museum in Philadelphia, if marked at all, were embossed "Museum" (Oliver, *Portraits of John and Abigail Adams*, p. 130; *The Monticello Family: Catalogue of an Exhibition Held at the University of Virginia Museum of Fine Arts, April 12–May 13, 1960* [Charlottesville, Va., 1960], pp. 8–9, 12–13).

[10]*Independent Chronicle*, Sept. 13, 20, 27, 1804; Sellers, *Charles Willson Peale*, 2: 166, 178, 190–91.

the size of his son's silhouette as good for framing;[11] so some admirers of the president who could not afford, or did not have an opportunity to purchase, an engraved print or a silver medal could display a pleasing shadow likeness. In any event, many of Jefferson's contemporaries must have had the opportunity to own or to see one of the Raphaelle Peale's well-cut silhouettes of President Jefferson taken from life in late June or early July 1804.[12]

[11] Peale to Jefferson, June 15, 1804, Jefferson Papers, Lib. Cong.

[12] Reproductions of two other examples of silhouettes of Jefferson that may have been contemporaneous with his presidency have been found, but little is known about either. Gaillard Hunt, in *The First Forty Years of Washington Society, Portrayed by the Family Letters of Mrs. Samuel Harrison Smith* (New York, 1906), facing p. 60, published a small silhouette of Jefferson together with similar silhouettes of James and Dolley Madison. They were identified only as "silhouettes from life," and Hunt gave no indication of ownership. An example of this has not been found. Another silhouette of Jefferson, by William Bache, was published in Alice Van Leer Carrick, *Shades of Our Ancestors: American Profiles and Profilists* (Boston, 1928), p. 64. This example was taken from William Bache's scrapbook owned by one of his descendants, and its authenticity as a work by Bache seems established. When it was cut, or whether it was taken from life, is not known. Bache was working in Philadelphia as early as 1793; he was in Richmond in 1804 and in Salem in 1808. No evidence has been found of Bache's silhouette of Jefferson being offered to the public.

Silhouettes purporting to be of Jefferson and John Adams made in 1789 by "Millette" were published accompanying an article by Wendell D. Garrett, "The Monumental Friendship of Jefferson and Adams," *Historic Preservation* 28, no. 2 (April–June 1976): 28, and on the cover of that issue. The silhouettes are in the Metropolitan Museum of Art. Robert G. Stewart, curator, National Portrait Gallery, Smithsonian Institution, has concluded, based on research by the National Portrait Gallery, that the silhouettes are fictitious and that "Millette" was a fictitious person. See Stewart's letter to the editor, *Historic Preservation* 28, no. 4 (Oct.-Dec., 1976): 47. I am in full agreement that these silhouettes must be rejected.

CHAPTER XI

Images on Display

THIS ART I THINK WILL MAKE BUT LITTLE PROGRESS IN the World," John Adams wrote to Abigail after viewing Mrs. Wells's waxworks in Philadelphia in May 1777.[1] Adams may have been correct; but the popularity of waxworks continued, and like most great men of his age, Adams himself was reproduced in wax.[2] So also was Jefferson.

A new museum of waxwork, exhibiting at Snow's Hotel, 69 Broadway, in New York City in 1804 advertised "a large and elegant collection of Wax-Work, consisting of fifty-six figures, as large as life," including "His Excellency Thomas Jefferson, President of the United States." Nicholas and Elnathan Street, the proprietors,

[1] John Adams to his wife, May 10, 1777, L. H. Butterfield, ed., *Adams Family Correspondence* (Cambridge, Mass., 1963), 2: 235. Rachel Lovell Wells was the sister of Patience Lovell Wright, who has been credited with originating the spectacle of life-sized figures of well-known contemporaries made in wax with great attention to detail and fidelity to nature. See Charles Coleman Sellers, *Benjamin Franklin in Portraiture* (New Haven, 1962), pp. 85, 426–27.

[2] Oliver, *Portraits of John and Abigail Adams*, p. 214.

heralded it as "the best collection of Wax-Figures ever exhibited in America." Admission for adults was one quarter of a dollar, half price for children. The next year in Georgetown, Moulthrop and Bishop opened "a new collection of Wax Figures, superior to any ever exhibited in America." Their notice in the Washington *National Intelligencer* employed the boldest print to advertise a display of the duel between Aaron Burr and Alexander Hamilton, but they also announced that their exhibition included "a striking likeness of Thomas Jefferson, President of the United States."[3]

The figures that filled these waxwork exhibits have long since disappeared, and there is little evidence upon which to judge their merit. That many Americans saw representations of Jefferson in such exhibitions is easier to document than what they saw. The glowing descriptions of promoters, however, were not always confirmed by viewers. "The wax work at Cambridge was of the ordinary kind and strangely placed," observed the Reverend William Bentley. "However, Mr. Jefferson was obliged to take his place at the head."[4]

Another means of displaying the images of public figures was the large transparent painting, in which form Jefferson's portrait appeared as early as his vice-presidency. In an evening illumination on July 4, 1797, the Panorama on Greenwich Street in New York City exhibited a transparent painting depicting the signing of the Declaration of Independence. The painting was described as "executed by a celebrated artist from original Paintings," but the artist

[3] *Weekly Museum* (New York), Mar. 3, 1804, advertisement in Gottesman, *Arts and Crafts in New York, 1800–1804*, pp. 91–92; *National Intelligencer*, Feb. 27, 1805. Reuben Moulthrop, an artist and modeler in wax, had exhibited figures of Washington, Adams, and others in New York (Oliver, *Portraits of John and Abigail Adams*, p. 214).

[4] Entry for Sept. 1, 1803, *The Diary of William Bentley, D.D., Pastor of the East Church, Salem, Massachusetts*, 3 vols. (Salem, Mass., 1911), 3: 40.

and the paintings were not identified. After Jefferson's election to the presidency, the display of transparent paintings of his portrait became common at July 4 celebrations in New York. At the first such commemoration after his inauguration, the Mount Vernon Garden, adjoining the Mount Vernon Theatre on Leonard Street near Broadway, illuminated a transparent "portrait of Thomas Jefferson, president of the United States, ornamented by geniuses."[5]

On the same occasion Waldron's Museum in New York illuminated an eight-by-five-foot full-length transparent painting of Jefferson.[6] This exhibition must have been particularly successful, for it was repeated on the following Christmas evening and on New Year's evening. The announcement of the showing proclaimed that Jefferson was "represented in the attitude in which he expressed that never to be forgotten sentence 'We are all Republicans we are all Federalists.' Every true Republican attached from principle to the name of Jefferson, cannot but be delighted in viewing the exact resemblance of a man so high in their estimation."[7] The measurements of this transparent painting suggest that it may have been drawn from Caleb Boyle's oil painting of Jefferson displayed in the Shakespeare Gallery in New York (fig. 58). But whether Boyle's likeness or not, the "exact resemblance" of the transparent painting claimed by the promoters may be questioned.

Boyle's oil painting of Jefferson must have been seen by numerous New Yorkers. A notice in the *New-York Evening Post*, April 3, 1802, advertised a full-length portrait of Jefferson "as large as Life . . . now exhibiting in the Shakespeare Gallery."[8] The catalogue of

[5] *Weekly Museum*, July 1, 1797, in Gottesman, *Arts and Crafts in New York, 1777–1799*, p. 32; *Commercial Advertiser*, July 3, 1801. See also issue of July 2, 1803.

[6] *American Citizen*, June 30, 1801.

[7] *New-York Evening Post*, Dec. 21, 1801, in Gottesman, *Arts and Crafts in New York, 1800–1804*, pp. 44–45.

[8] Ibid., p. 19.

Fig. 58. Painting of Jefferson by Caleb Boyle, 1801

that gallery's exhibits in 1802 described it as: "Painted by Boyle, of New York 1801. Size of Canvas, 5 by 8 feet high. In the background is a view of the celebrated Rock Bridge in Virginia."[9] Boyle's life-size painting, however, was not drawn from life; it was a made-up portrait in which the head of Jefferson was taken from David Edwin's 1800 engraving after Rembrandt Peale — the most widely copied engraving of Jefferson circulating at the time Boyle painted his large canvas. An engraving of the Rock Bridge in Virginia from a drawing by Isaac Weld, Jr., was also available for copying. Published by John Stockdale, December 5, 1798, it was included in Weld's account of his travels in America from 1795 to 1797 published by Stockdale in London in 1799. Three editions of the work had appeared by 1800, and it must have been easily accessible for Boyle to copy as a background.[10]

While visitors to the Shakespeare Gallery in New York saw only Jefferson's portrait derived from an engraving, patrons of Peale's Museum in Philadelphia were more fortunate. Charles Willson Peale's life portrait of Jefferson (Appendix, plate II) was part of the permanent exhibition, and Rembrandt Peale's work was also at times on display. Fortunate indeed were the visitors to Peale's Museum on the evening of March 3, 1805 — the eve of Jefferson's second inaugural. In an evening illumination of the museum they

[9]*Longworth's American Almanac, New-York Register and City Directory for the Twenty-Seventh Year of American Independence* (New York, 1802), quoted in John Jay Ide, "A Discovery in Early American Portraiture," *Antiques* 25 (1934): 99. The copy at the New-York Historical Society contains this information, but it is not included in the copy in the Rare Book Division, Library of Congress.

[10]Isaac Weld, Jr., *Travels through the States of North America, and the Provinces of Upper and Lower Canada, during the Years 1795, 1796, and 1797*, 2 vols. (3d ed., London, 1800), 1: 221. In the first edition published in one volume (London, 1799), the Rock Bridge print appeared as the frontispiece. Also available, but clearly not copied by Boyle, was "A View of the Natural Bridge in Virginia" published in *The Columbian Magazine*, Sept. 1787.

saw both a gigantic transparency portrait of Jefferson and the recently completed life portrait of the president by Rembrandt Peale — the second portrait for which Jefferson had sat for that talented artist (Appendix, plate VIII). Peale had put the final touches on his new work little more than a month before this exhibition.[11] Rarely had the public anywhere had the opportunity to view so recent an interpretation of the president's portrait.

Before leaving Washington, Peale had advertised that "those gentlemen who are desirous of obtaining copies of the Portrait of the President, just finished, by REMBRANDT PEALE, are requested to call at his Painting Room at Miss Dashields, Pennsylvania avenue, where the picture can be seen for a few days, during which R. Peale will remain in this city." How many persons called to view the portrait is not recorded; nor is it known how many orders for copies he received, but only one copy is known to survive. Surprisingly, the portrait was never engraved during the nineteenth century.[12]

Notices in newspapers in Washington, Philadelphia, New York, and other cities document many public displays of Jefferson's portraits, but less well-advertised exhibitions of his likeness may also have taken place, particularly in smaller towns. The Reverend William Bentley, describing the decoration of the Meeting House in Salem on the Fourth of July 1804, observed: "The front of the Pulpit was decorated with the arms of the United States, inscribed American Independence. Below was an elegant engraving of Jefferson, who was also displayed on the front gallery, on glass in gold. On his right hand was Washington and on his left a beautiful figure

[11] Sellers, *Charles Willson Peale*, 2: 190. Jefferson sat for Rembrandt Peale on Jan. 23, 24, and 31, 1805, and the portrait was completed on the last of these sittings (Charles Willson Peale to Raphaelle, Rubens, and Sophonisba Peale, Jan. 30–Feb. 1, 1805, Charles Willson Peale letter book, Am. Phil. Soc.; Bush, "Life Portraits of Jefferson," p. 72).

[12] *National Intelligencer*, Jan. 30, Feb. 1, 6, 8, 11, 13, 15, 1805; Bush, "Life Portraits of Jefferson," p. 72.

Fig. 59. Jefferson portrait on glass, engraved in gold by A. B. Doolittle, 1803

of Liberty. On the sides of the Arms of the State were in Gold, Madison and Gallatin."[13] A print of the engraving of Jefferson by Desnoyers (see fig. 27) once owned by Bentley survives today, suggesting that this may have been the engraving to which he referred.[14] The Jefferson portrait on glass almost certainly was the profile engraved in gold by A. B. Doolittle (fig. 59) in 1803, for no

[13] *The Diary of William Bentley*, 3: 96.

[14] The print is at the Essex Institute, Salem, on deposit from the Peabody Museum of Salem. The files of the Essex Institute record the tradition that the print was given to Bentley by Jefferson, but this has not been confirmed.

Fig. 60. Textile banner celebrating Jefferson's election in 1801

other Jefferson portrait on glass in gold is known. One of Doolittle's profiles of Jefferson hung at Monticello in Jefferson's time and hangs there again today.[15]

How many copies of this profile Doolittle may have made is not known. On three different occasions in late 1803 and early 1804

[15] Jefferson, "Catalogue of Paintings Etc. at Monticello," Jefferson Papers, Univ. of Va. Library; Bush, "Life Portraits of Jefferson," pp. 64–66.

Jefferson paid Doolittle for profiles, altogether buying seven profiles at five dollars each.[16] Whether these profiles were of Jefferson is not recorded, but it seems likely that at least some of them were. It has been assumed that it was for one of Doolittle's profiles that Elizabeth Trist thanked Jefferson in November 1804, writing to him from New Orleans: "Your likeness [delivered] by Mr. [Isaac] Briggs I received with pleasure it is exactly your self in short it elated the Spirits of us all to behold so perfect a resemblance of such a valued and dear friend, to me it is an inestimable treasure."[17] While this seems elaborate praise for the work of Doolittle, there is no other known likeness of Jefferson to which Mrs. Trist's remarks can apply.

Nearly all of the primitive art that may have been created by Jefferson's contemporaries to portray him has disappeared. One rare example can be seen today in the Smithsonian Institution, which has a textile banner measuring thirty by thirty-seven inches that may have been used in celebrating Jefferson's election victory in 1801. The banner is dominated by a crude portrait of Jefferson, embellished by stars and an eagle holding streamers proclaiming "T. Jefferson, President of the United States of America" and "John Adams is no More" (fig. 60). The use of the eagle and sixteen stars is suggestive of the print that accompanied William Durell's edition of Jefferson's first inaugural address (see fig. 6), but the drawing of Jefferson does not follow the Savage image that appeared in Durell's print.

It is impossible to recover all the representations of Jefferson that the people saw, but the images on public display exhibited a vast range of artistic abilities from the portraits by Rembrandt Peale to the banner by the unknown artist who hailed Jefferson's election.

[16]Jefferson, Account Books, Dec. 23, 1803, Jan. 7, Feb. 10, 1804, transcript by James A. Bear, Jr., Univ. of Va. Library; Bush, "Life Portraits of Jefferson," pp. 64, 66.

[17]Elizabeth Trist to Jefferson, Nov. 26, 1804, Jefferson Papers, Univ. of Va. Library.

CHAPTER XII

Portraits for the People

THE PRINTS WHICH HAVE BEEN OFFERED THE PUBLIC ARE such miserable caracatures," Jefferson said in 1802 in regard to the various engravings that had been made of his portraits.[1] Just how many of these prints he had seen is not known, though it is unlikely that he ever saw all of the prints that are published in this book. He must have seen the major engravings made by David Edwin and by Cornelius Tiebout, but in his criticism he more likely had in mind the numerous inaccurate copies that derived from them. He could hardly have avoided seeing some of the distorted versions of Edward Savage's portrait, which more than most other prints could be dismissed as miserable caricatures, and these may well have been uppermost in Jefferson's mind when he pronounced his bleak verdict. Yet even the best engravings by Edwin and by Tiebout were not accurate copies of Rembrandt Peale's portrait of 1800, as Peale himself disappointedly asserted. A full year after Jefferson's inauguration, the public still did not have access to an accurate copy of

[1] Jefferson to Martha Jefferson Randolph, April 3, 1802, Betts and Bear, eds., *Family Letters of Thomas Jefferson*, p. 221.

a portrait of the president. Most of the engravings that derived from Savage and most of the portraits of Jefferson that appeared in English prints and their derivatives showed a stern figure that may have been a product not merely of a lack of artistic skills but also of engravers' perceptions of an authority figure demanded by the presidential office. Unfortunately, many of the early indifferent engravings were recopied and republished throughout the course of Jefferson's presidency, and many people may never have seen a faithful depiction of him.

Despite the artistic deficiencies of many of the early Jefferson engravings and their persistent circulation, the period of Jefferson's administration brought important changes in the artistic quality of the portraits of Jefferson available to the public. The medallic portrait by John Reich after Houdon, which Jefferson and all who commented on it so much admired, marked the beginning of the transformation. This was followed by Saint-Mémin's superior engraving of his own life drawing in 1804. That both Reich and Saint-Mémin were European artists working in America reflected the backward state of the art of engraving in the United States that Rembrandt Peale earlier had so much deplored. Two English-born artists, Robert Field and David Edwin, contributed further to the progress made in engraving during the course of Jefferson's presidency, as seen in the beautiful engraving by Field in 1807 of Gilbert Stuart's 1805 portrait of Jefferson and in the 1809 engraving by Edwin of Stuart's medallion portrait. These examples visually reveal that the art of engraved portraiture was coming of age in the United States. Jefferson's role in this was limited to encouraging artists of every description, but the advance was a fitting tribute to the friend of the arts who occupied the presidential office. Although Jefferson had curtly dismissed the early engravings of him, he was pleased to present the medal by Reich and the engraving by Saint-Mémin; and the engraving by Edwin from Stuart's medallion portrait was a print that he admired immensely.

The appreciation by Americans of the art of engraving matured during the years of Jefferson's presidency. This is perhaps most evident in the fact that it was Stuart's image of Jefferson faithfully portrayed in Field's engraved print that became the most popular portrait of Jefferson and in subsequent years the predominant icon of the man of Monticello. Those who best knew Jefferson favored Stuart's likenesses, and public critics found Stuart's work unexcelled. "We scarcely ever saw a portrait from his pencil that could not be immediately identified," wrote one critic in 1800.[2] The fact that Field's print of Stuart's portrait could be purchased for one dollar made not only the president's image but also a work of art widely available to the public.

Jefferson's image never attracted the interest or the attention that Washington's commanded, but the examples provided in this book show that the people had access to far more portraits of President Jefferson than has been previously appreciated. The extent and variety of the separate engraved prints contemporaneous with Jefferson's presidency is impressive, even if the artistic merit of the early prints is not. The people saw portraits of the president in magazines and books — including the numerous editions of Jefferson's *Notes on the State of Virginia* — on medals, on pieces of Liverpool pottery ware, in silhouettes, in waxworks, and in other public displays. Together, these sources — sometimes disappointing, in other instances elegant — furnished the public with the visual image of the third president of the United States. These portraits for the people were evidence of the popular interest in the president and examples of the artistic efforts of Jefferson's America.

[2] *Aurora* (Philadelphia), July 16, 1800.

Catalogue

Note on Sources

Appendix: Sources of the People's Image

Credits

Index

Catalogue

THE FOLLOWING CATALOGUE LISTS ALL OF THE PRINTS and other images of Jefferson that have been identified as being available to the public during the period of Jefferson's presidency from 1801 to 1809. It does not include original portraits, drawings, or engravings that had no public circulation.

Each entry identifies where possible the engraver and the source from which it derives and indicates the size of the picture and any inscription which it bears. Engravings listed in David McNeely Stauffer's *American Engravers upon Copper and Steel* (2 vols., New York, 1907) and in Mantle Fielding's supplement to that work (Philadelphia, 1917) are identified by the numerical designation given in those works. The location indicates the copy from which the reproduction in this work has been made or the copy consulted if no reproduction is published.

The number preceding each item is used for all cross-references within the catalogue. This catalogue number should not be confused with the figure number, which is shown in the right-hand margin and indicates items illustrated in the text. Plate numbers refer to reproductions in the Appendix. Items mentioned in the text but not illustrated are indicated by page references in the right-hand margin.

Prints

Cat. No.

1. Thomas Jefferson. Stipple engraving by James Akin (ca. 1733–1846) and William Harrison, Jr., Philadelphia, 1800, after oil portrait by Charles Willson Peale (1741–1827) painted in 1791. Size: 5 3/8 x 4 1/4 in., oval. Inscribed: "Painted by C. W. Peale 1791. Engraved by Akin & Harrison Junr. / Thomas Jefferson Esqr. / Vice-President of the United States & / President of the American Philosophical Society. /Philada. Pub. by A & H Junr. Jany. 10th 1800." Stauffer no. 17. Atwater Kent Museum, Philadelphia. Pl. II; Fig. 1

2. Thomas Jefferson. Mezzotint by Edward Savage (1761–1817), Philadelphia, 1800, after portrait by Edward Savage, 1800. Size: 9 7/16 x 7 15/16 in. Inscribed: "E Savage Pinx & sc — Philada Published June 1, 1800 / Thomas Jefferson." Stauffer no. 2746. The Metropolitan Museum of Art, Bequest of Charles Allen Munn, 1924. Fig. 3

3. Thomas Jefferson. Stipple engraving by John Scoles, 1801, after no. 2. Size: 5 5/16 x 3 3/8 in., oval in lined rectangle. "T. Jefferson." inscribed in rectangle below portrait. Signed "Scoles, sc." Stauffer no. 2787. Published as frontispiece in three editions of Thomas Jefferson, *Notes on the State of Virginia*: (1) third American edition, Newark, N.J.: printed by Pennington & Gould, 1801; (2) third American edition, New York: printed by M. L. & W. A. Davis for Furman & Loudon, 1801; (3) fourth American edition, New York: T. B. Jansen & Co. & G. Jansen & Co., 1801. Fig. 4

4. Thomas Jefferson. Stipple engraving by Enoch G. Gridley, 1801, after no. 2. Size: 5 5/16 × 3 5/16 in., oval in lined rectangle. "T. Jefferson." inscribed in rectangle below portrait. Published as frontispiece in Thomas Jefferson, *Notes on the State of Virginia*, eighth American edition, Boston: printed by David Carlisle . . . 1801. Found in signed and unsigned states. Virginia Historical Society copy inscribed "Gridley sc." Fig. 5

5. Thomas Jefferson. Wood engraving by unknown artist, 1801, after no. 2. Size: 3 1/16 x 2 1/2 in., oval. Eagle and sixteen stars above portrait. Inscribed: "Thomas Jefferson, / President of the United States." Published as frontispiece in *Speech of Thomas Jefferson, President of the United States; Delivered in the Senate Chamber of the Capitol, the 4th of March at 12 O'Clock*, New York: printed by William Durell, No. 106, Maiden-Lane, 1801. Rare Book Division, Library of Congress. Fig. 6

6. Thomas Jefferson. Stipple engraving by unknown artist. Size: 3 7/16 x 2 3/4 in., oval. Inscribed: "Thos. Jefferson. / President of the United States." Fielding no. 1827. Published in James Hardie, *The New Universal Biographical Dictionary, and American Remembrancer of Departed Merit*, 4 vols., New York, 1801–5, facing p. 65 in vol. 1 (1801) and as frontispiece in vol. 3 (1805). The Metropolitan Museum of Art, Bequest of Charles Allen Munn, 1924. Fig. 2

   Published earlier, inscribed "Thos. Jefferson," in Charles Smith, *The Gentleman's Political Pocket Almanac, for the Year 1797* (New York, 1796).

7. Thomas Jefferson. Stipple engraving by David Edwin (1776–1841), after oil portrait by Rembrandt Peale Pl. IV (1778–1860) painted in 1800. Size: 11 5/16 x 9 1/16 in. Appeared in three states, inscribed: (1) "R. Peale Pinx — D. Edwin sc / Thomas Jefferson Esqr. / Vice President of the United States. / Published by J. Savage 1800"; (2) with "Vice" erased (as illustrated); (3) same as second state with Fig. 7 publisher and date erased. Stauffer no. 787. Boston Museum of Fine Arts.

8. Thomas Jefferson. Stipple engraving by Cornelius Tiebout (ca. 1773–1832), Philadelphia, 1800, after no. 7. Size: 5 7/8 x 4 11/16 in., oval. Inscribed: "Tiebout sc. / Thomas Jefferson, / Vice President of the U.S. / Published by D. Kennedy No. 228 Market St." Stauffer no. 3180. Emmet Collection no. 1371, Manuscripts and Archives Division, The New York Public Library. Fig. 10

   Also published in *The Literary Magazine, and American Register* 2 (Philadelphia; September 1804): facing p. 413, with last two lines of inscriptions cut off before binding. Virginia State Library. Fig. 12

9. Thomas Jefferson. Stipple engraving by Cornelius Tiebout, Philadelphia, published after 1800 and before 1805, after no. 8. Size: 9 1/16 x 7 1/8 in., oval. Inscribed: "R. Peale Pinxt. C. Tiebout Sculpt. / Thomas Jefferson. / Published by A. Day No. 38 Chesnut St. Philada." Emmet Collection no. 10226, Manuscripts and Archives Division, The New York Public Library. Fig. 11

10. Thomas Jefferson. Stipple engraving by Enoch G. Gridley, Boston, 1801, after no. 7. Size: 11 3/16 x 9 in. Inscribed: "E G Gridley Sc. State St. Boston. / Thomas Jefferson Esq." Fielding no. 531. The Mabel Brady Garvan Collection, Yale University Art Gallaery. Fig. 8

11. Thomas Jefferson. Stipple and line engraving by John Norman (1748–1817), [ca. 1801], after no. 7. Size: 14 x 9 1/4 in. Inscribed: "J Norman Sc / Thomas Jefferson / President of the United States." The Mabel Brady Garvan Collection, Yale University Art Gallery. Fig. 9

12. Thomas Jefferson. Stipple engraving by Johannes Senn (1780–1861), 1801, after no. 7. Size: 3 1/16 x 2 3/8 in. Inscribed: "R Peale Pinx — J Senn Sculps / Thomas Jefferson." Published in *Almanac Americain pour l'Annee 1802*, Philadelphia, [1801], facing p. 211. Rare Book Division, Library of Congress. Fig. 13

13. Thomas Jefferson. Stipple engraving by Benjamin Tanner (1775–1848), Philadelphia, 1801, derived from no. 7. Size: 3 3/16 x 2 3/8 in., oval in lined rectangle. "T. Jefferson." inscribed in rectangle below portrait. Signed: "B. Tanner, sc. / Published by M. Carey." Stauffer no. 3094. Published as frontispiece in *Speech of Thomas Jefferson, President of the United States, Delivered at His Instalment, March 4, 1801, at the City of Washington* . . . , Philadelphia: printed by Cochran & McLaughlin, for Mathew Carey, 118, Market-street, 1801. Rare Book Division, The New York Public Library. Fig. 16

Also published as frontispiece in Thomas Jefferson, *Notes on the State of Virginia*, Trenton: printed by Wilson & Blackwell, for Mathew Carey, No. 118 Market-St., Philadelphia, 1803. Fig. 15

Portrait, without inscription, at top of broadside entitled *Speech of Thomas Jefferson, President of the United States, Delivered at His Instalment, March 4, 1801, at the City of Washington*, third edition, Philadelphia: published by Mathew Carey, H. Maxwell, printer, [1801]. Printed on both paper and silk textile; size of broadside: 19 ½ x 15 5/16 in. Massachusetts Historical Society. Fig. 17

14. Thomas Jefferson. Stipple engraving by unknown artist, Dublin, 1801, derived from no. 13. Size: 2 x 1 ¾ in., oval. Inscribed: "T. Jefferson. / President of the / United States of America." Published in *Walker's Hibernian Magazine: or, Compendium of Entertaining Knowledge. For April, 1801*, Dublin: printed by Richard Gibson, 1801, facing p. 193. Library of Congress. Fig. 19

15. Thomas Jefferson. Stipple engraving by John Kay (1742–1826), Edinburgh, 1801, after no. 13 or no. 14. Size: 2 ½ x 2 ¼ in., oval in lined rectangle. Inscribed: "Thomas Jefferson / President of the United States / of America / J. Kay 1801." William J. Campbell Collection, American Philosophical Society. Fig. 20

16. Thomas Jefferson. Stipple engraving by unknown artist, London, 1801, after no. 7 or one of its derivatives. Size: 4 5/16 x 3 5/16 in., oval. Inscribed: "Painted by Stuart in America. / Thos. Jefferson, / President / of the United States of America. / Sold & Published August 1, 1801, by Edwd. Orme, 59 New Bond Street, London." University of Virginia Library. Fig. 22

Published in another state with publisher altered to read "Published by J Sewell Cornhill June 1 1802," William J. Campbell Collection, American Philosophical Society. This state was published with "European Magazine" inscribed above the portrait in *The European Magazine, and London Review* 41 (May 1802): facing p. 339. The New York Public Library. Fig. 24

17. Thomas Jefferson. Stipple engraving by unknown artist, London, 1801, after no. 7 or one of its derivatives. Size: 3 $\frac{1}{4}$ x 2 $\frac{1}{2}$ in., oval. Inscribed: "Thomas Jefferson Esqr. / Published Oct. 1, 1801, by Vernor & Hood, Poultry." Published in *The Monthly Visitor, and New Family Magazine* 14 (London; September 1801). The New York Public Library. Fig. 21

18. Thomas Jefferson. Stipple engraving by Friedrich Wilhelm Nettling (1793–1824), Leipzig, 1801, after no. 16. Size: 4 $\frac{5}{16}$ x 3 $\frac{3}{8}$ in., oval. Inscribed: "gem. v. Stuart in America. — gest. v. F. W. Nettling L. 1801. / Thos. Jefferson / President der vereinigten Staaten in America." "No. 28" is inscribed in upper right corner. University of Virginia Library. Fig. 23

19. Thomas Jefferson. Stipple engraving, full-length standing, by David Edwin, Philadelphia, 1801, after no. 7. Size: 20 x 13 in. Inscribed: "D. Edwin Fecit / Publish'd by G. Helmbold Junr. / Philada. 1801." Stauffer no. 788. Virginia Historical Society. Fig. 28

    Second state, plate materially altered, inscribed: "D. Edwin Fecit / Jefferson." Historical Society of Pennsylvania. Fig. 29

20. Thomas Jefferson. Stipple engraving by Enoch G. Gridley, Boston, 1802, after no. 7 or one of its derivatives. Size: 3 $\frac{5}{16}$ x 2 $\frac{1}{4}$ in., oval in lined rectangle. "T. Jefferson." inscribed in rectangle below portrait. Signed: "Gridley sc. / Published by H. Sprague." Stauffer no. 1180. Published as frontispiece in Thomas Jefferson, *Notes on the State of Virginia*, ninth American edition, Boston: printed by H. Sprague, no. 44 Marlboro Street, 1802. Virginia State Library. Fig. 18

21. Thomas Jefferson. Stipple engraving by Cornelius Tiebout, Philadelphia, 1801, after oil portrait by Rembrandt Peale Pl. IV painted in 1800. Size: 10 $\frac{15}{16}$ x 8 $\frac{3}{4}$ in. Inscribed: "R. Peale Pinxt. — C. Tiebout Sculpt. / Thomas Jefferson. / President of the United States. / [twelve lines in two columns from Declaration of Independence] / Philadelphia Published by M. Carey No. 118 Market St. Feb. 20th 1801 Copy right Secured." Stauffer no. 3182. National Portrait Gallery, Smithsonian Institution. Fig. 25

22. Thomas Jefferson. Stipple engraving, full-length standing, by Cornelius Tiebout, Philadelphia, 1801, after no. 21. Size: 19 $\frac{7}{8}$ x 13 in. Inscribed: "Thomas Jefferson / President of the United States. / Published by A. Day No. 38 Chesnut Street Philada." Stauffer no. 3181. Library of Congress. Fig. 30

    Second state inscribed: "Peale Del. Published by W. H. Morgan, Philada. Tiebout, Sc. / Thomas Jefferson / President of the United States." The New York Public Library.

    Third state, publisher changed to "Pub. by William Smith No. 702 So. 3d St. Phila."

23. Thomas Jefferson. Stipple engraving by Auguste-Gaspard-Louis Boucher Desnoyers (1779–1857), Paris, 1801, from crayon drawing by Bouch dated 1801 and drawn from no. 21. Size: 9 $\frac{3}{4}$ x 7 $\frac{3}{4}$ in. Inscribed: "Bouch delt. Deposé à la Bibliothèque Nationale le 25 Fructidor an 9. Aug. Desnoyers Sculpt. / Thomas Jefferson. / President des Etats unis de l'Amerique an 1801. / Se trouve chez le Cn. Martin, Md. d'Estampes, Rue Fossés, Montmartre N. 27." Emmet Collection no. 2529, Manuscripts and Archives Division, The New York Public Library. Fig. 27

24. Thomas Jefferson. Stipple engraving by William Harrison, Jr., Philadelphia, 1801, after no. 21. Size: 4 $\frac{3}{4}$ x 3 $\frac{13}{16}$ in., oval. Inscribed: "Engraved by Harrison Junr. / Thomas Jefferson." Stauffer no. 1288. Published as frontispiece in Thomas Jefferson, *Notes on the State of Virginia*, Philadelphia: R. T. Rawle, Publisher, John Thompson, Printer, June 1801. Fig. 26

25. Thomas Jefferson. Mezzotint by Charles-Balthazar-Julien Févret de Saint-Mémin (1770–1852), Washington, D.C., 1805, from original drawing by Saint-Mémin, 1804. Size: 2 $\frac{15}{16}$ x 2 $\frac{7}{16}$ in., oval. Inscribed: "Th: Jefferson / St. Memin delt. & sct." Rare Book Room, Princeton University Library. Pl. V Fig. 36

    Another version, round, diameter 2 $\frac{3}{16}$ in., inscribed: "St. Mn. ft." Engraved for Thomas Jefferson, 1804. Thomas Jefferson Papers, Harold Jefferson Coolidge Collection, University of Virginia Library. Fig. 35

26. Thomas Jefferson. Stipple engraving by Thomas Gimbrede (1781–1832), New York, 1809, after no. 25. Size: 7 5/8 x 5 3/4 in. Inscribed: "Desd. & Engd. by T. Gimbrede N.Y. / Thos. Jefferson the Pride of America / Retired March 4, 1809." William J. Campbell Collection, American Philosophical Society. Fig. 37

27. Thomas Jefferson. Stipple engraving by Robert Field (ca. 1769–1819), Boston, 1807, bust only, of Gilbert Stuart's (1755–1828) replica for James Bowdoin III of his 1805 oil Pl. VI portrait of Jefferson. Size: 5 7/8 x 5 1/8 in., oval in lined rectangle. Inscribed: "G. Stuart. Pinxit — R. Field. Sculpsit. / Thomas Jefferson. / Boston, Published by Robert Field, March 14th 1807." Stauffer no. 1001. The Metropolitan Museum of Art, Bequest of Charles Allen Munn, 1924. Fig. 38

28. Thomas Jefferson. Stipple engraving by David Edwin, 1809, from drawing by William Russell Birch (1755–1834) of medallion profile by Gilbert Stuart, 1805. Vignette, size: 2 3/4 x Pl. VII 1 7/8 in. Inscribed: "Jefferson. / G. Stuart Pinx / W. Birch delin. D. Edwin sc. 1809. / Copy Right Secured according to Law." Stauffer no. 789. University of Virginia Library. Fig. 39

29. Goddess of liberty holding portrait of Thomas Jefferson. Engraving by unknown artist. Size: 14 5/8 x 17 3/8 in. Inscribed: "Pubd. Salem Jany. 15th 1807 Price two Dollars." Also inscribed:

> Explanation. In the Center is the Goddess of Liberty sitting on the Globe supporting on her knee with one Hand the Portrait of THOMAS JEFFERSON, President of the United States. with the other she is pointing him out as the Favorite of the People. Round her head are the sixteen Stars to represent the different States. On the Monument is the Portrait of the late General GEORGE WASHINGTON. The eyes of the Goddess are fixed thereon in remembrance of past services. The rays of glory from the sixteen Stars strike their splendid beams on each Portrait. The emblems of Monarchy are under the foot of the Goddess. At the foot of the Monument is the Genius of Peace, presenting the Olive Branch to the Portrait of Gen. Washington. The Genius of Gratitude is crowning him with Laurels. The Back Ground is distinguished by the Rays

of Glory, shining on a vessel at a distance, to denote the protection of Commerce. — The Supporters of the Work are: No. 1 Brittania No. 2 Neptune No. 3 Fame No. 4 Abundance

The Mabel Brady Garvan Collection, Yale University Art Gallery. Fig. 14

30. "A New Display of the United States." Engraved by Amos Doolittle, New Haven, 1803. Bust of Jefferson surrounded by coats of arms of the states and inscribed: "Thomas Jefferson, President of the United States, Supporter of Liberty, True Republican and Friend of the Rights of Man." Not located. This description is taken from William A. Beardsley, "An Old New Haven Engraver and His Work: Amos Doolittle," *Papers of the New Haven Colony Historical Society* 8 (1914): 144.

Caricatures

31. "The Times; a Political Portrait." Engraving by unknown artist, unsigned and undated [ca. 1795–97]. Size: 12 1/4 x 17 3/4 in. Inscribed: "Triumph Government: perish all its enemies. — Traitors, be warned: justice though slow, is sure." New-York Historical Society. p. 112

32. "The Providential Detection." Etching and engraving by unknown artist; watermark 1794, [ca. 1797]. Jefferson kneeling before the altar of Gallic despotism. Size: 16 1/4 x 14 in. Library Company of Philadelphia; American Antiquarian Society. p. 112

33. "The Prairie Dog Sickened at the sting of the Hornet, or a Diplomatic Puppet exhibiting his Deceptions!" Etching (colored impression) by James Akin, [Newburyport, Mass., 1806]. Size: 11 15/16 x 15 15/16 in. An emaciated dog with the head of Jefferson, stung by a hornet with the head of Napoleon. Signed: "J Akin fect." Library of Congress. p. 114

34. "Look on This Picture, and on This." Etching and engraving by an unknown artist, New York, June 1807. Oval portraits

of Washington and Jefferson; Jefferson portrait after no. 27. Oval portraits, 4 ⅞ x 3 15/16 in., on rectangle 9 ⅞ x 12 ¼ in. Stauffer no. 1005. The New-York Historical Society. Fig. 52

35. "The happy Effects of that Grand Systom of shutting Ports against the English!!" Engraving (colored impression) by Issac and/or George Cruikshank, 1808. Size: 8 ⅜ x 13 ⅛ in. Signed: "Cruikshank, Pubd. Walker 7 Cornhill Octr. 1, 1808." Thomas Jefferson Memorial Foundation, Monticello. Fig. 53

36. "King Quilldriver's Experiments on National Defence." 1808. Signed: "Peter Pencil [pseud.] fecit." Facsimile at the Historical Society of Pennsylvania. Print not located. p. 118

37. [Untitled cartoon]. Etching by unknown artist, unsigned and undated [ca. 1808–9]; in three frames. Size: 17 x 12 ⅞ in. Written in ink above frame showing Jefferson on the only copy located: "An old Philosopher teaching his mad Son economical Projects." The Free Library of Philadelphia. Fig. 54

38. "Intercourse or Impartial Dealings." Signed: "Peter Pencil [pseud.] fecit 1809." Size: 11 ⅜ x 13 ¾ in. Etching and stipple printed with sepia ink. Jefferson image after no. 7. The Houghton Library, Harvard University. Fig. 55

39. "Non Intercourse or Dignified Retirement." Signed: "Peter Pencill [pseud.] fecit 1809." Size: 11 ¾ x 13 ¾ in. Etching and stipple printed with sepia ink. Jefferson image after no. 7. The Houghton Library, Harvard University. Fig. 56

Transfers on Earthenware

40. Thomas Jefferson. Transfer design on earthenware, Liverpool, [ca. 1801], after no. 16. Same as on no. 46. Pitcher, 7 ¾ in. high, portrait in oval surrounded by garland entwined by ribbon with the names of the first fifteen states. Inscribed: "Thomas Jefferson, / President of the United States of America." Opposite side: oval within fifteen stars and fifteen states containing same verse as on no. 41. National Museum of History and Technology, Smithsonian Institution. Fig. 41

41. Thomas Jefferson. Transfer design on earthenware, Liverpool, [ca. 1801], after no. 16. Same as on no. 42. Pitcher, 6 5/8 in. high, portrait in oval, inscribed: "Thomas Jefferson, / President of the United States of America." Verse on opposite side: Fig. 43

> O Liberty thou Goddess!
> heav'nly bright,
> Profuse of bliss,
> and pregnant with delight,
> Eternal pleasures
> in thy presence reign,
> and smiling plenty leads
> thy wanton train.

Peabody Museum of Salem, Massachusetts.

42. Thomas Jefferson. Transfer design on earthenware, Liverpool, [ca. 1801], after no. 16. Same as on no. 41. Mug 4 5/8 in. high, portrait in oval, inscribed: "Thomas Jefferson, / President of the United States of America." National Museum of History and Technology, Smithsonian Institution. Fig. 44

43. Thomas Jefferson. Transfer design on earthenware, Liverpool, [ca. 1801], after no. 16. Pitcher, 6 5/8 in. high, portrait in oval with border containing the names of the first fifteen states and banner inscribed: "Thomas Jefferson, President of the United States of America." Unnamed American ship on opposite side. Peabody Museum of Salem, Massachusetts. Fig. 45

44. Thomas Jefferson. Transfer design on earthenware, Liverpool, [ca. 1801]. Pitcher, 9 1/4 in. high, circular wreath of olive branches surmounted by portrait of Jefferson framed by two doves with spreading wings. Inside wreath is the verse:

> Hail Columbia happy land
> Hail ye patriotic band
> Who late oppos'd oppressive laws
> And now stand firm in freedom's cause
> Rejoice for now the storm is gone
> Columbia owns her chosen son
> The rights of man shall be our boast

And jefferson out fav'rite toast
Republicans behold your chief
He comes to give your fears relief
Now arm'd in virtue firm and true
Looks for support to Heaven and you Fig. 49

Opposite side: an emblem of the United States. Under spout: eagle, shield, and stars. National Museum of History and Technology, Smithsonian Institution.

45. Thomas Jefferson. Transfer design on earthenware, Liverpool, 1801. Pitcher, 7 3/4 in. high, portrait in oval with wreath of states; above it: "We are all Republicans — all Federalists." Below portrait: "Thomas Jefferson / President of the United States / of America / 1801." Opposite side: emblem of the United States. National Museum of History and Technology, Smithsonian Institution. Fig. 51

46. Thomas Jefferson. Transfer design on earthenware, Liverpool, 1802. Same as on no. 40. Pitcher, 9 in. high, portrait in oval surrounded by garland entwined by ribbon with the names of the first fifteen states. Inscribed: "Thomas Jefferson, / President of the United States of America." Opposite side: unnamed American ship and scroll with words "Success to Trade." Under the spout: a representation of the Seal of the United States and "Peace, Commerce and honest Friendship with all Nations, Entangling Alliances with none — Jefferson / Anno Domini 1802." Thomas Greg Collection, City of Manchester Art Galleries, Manchester, England. Fig. 42

47. [Unknown figure]. Transfer design on earthenware, Liverpool, [ca. 1800]. Pitcher, 9 5/8 in. high, full-length figure with document in his hand; entitled "Jefferson." Opposite side: profile portrait of Washington in a medallion surrounded by palms, and the words: "He in Glory, America in Tears." Under the spout: initials "M.B.C." in wreath above eagle, shield, and stars. National Museum of History and Technology, Smithsonian Institution. Fig. 40

48. [Unknown figure]. Transfer design on earthenware, [Liverpool]. Pitcher. Portrait of unknown person entitled: "Thomas

Jefferson / President of the United States / of America." Original unlocated; photograph in possession of Alan Smith, Manchester, England. Fig. 47

49. [Cartoon]. Transfer design on earthenware, Liverpool, [ca. 1808–9]. Pitcher, 8 3/4 in. high. Under spout, a cartoon showing cow being milked by figure labeled "Jefferson," while "John Bull" holds the horns of the cow and "Bonaparte" pulls its tail. On front side: "The Farmers Arms"; opposite side: "The Farm Yard." National Museum of History and Technology, Smithsonian Institution. Fig. 50

Medals

50. Thomas Jefferson. Medallic portrait, Indian peace medal, by John Reich (1768–1833), Philadelphia, 1801, after bust by Jean-Antoine Houdon (1741–1828), 1789. Inscribed: obverse, "Th. Jefferson President of the U.S. A.D. 1801"; reverse, "Peace and Friendship." Struck in copper, pewter, and silver in three sizes: small (54–55 mm.), medium (76–77 mm.), and large (101–105 mm.). Example illustrated is 101 mm. hollow silver. American Numismatic Society. Pl. I Fig. 33 Fig. 34

51. Thomas Jefferson. Medallic portrait by John Reich, Philadelphia, 1802, after bust by Jean-Antoine Houdon, 1789. Inscribed: obverse, "Th. Jefferson President of the U.S. 4 March 1801"; reverse, "Under His Wing Is Protection / To Commemorate / July 4, 1776." Struck in silver and pewter. Size: 45 mm. Example illustrated is solid silver. American Numismatic Society. Pl. I Fig. 31 Fig. 32

Silhouette

52. Thomas Jefferson. Silhouette by Raphaelle Peale (1774–1825), [Washington, D.C., 1804]. Size: 2 7/8 x 1 3/4 in., cut from paper 4 1/2 x 3 7/8 in. Embossed with the name "PEALE" immediately under the bust. Thomas Jefferson Memorial Foundation, Monticello. Fig. 57

Others

53. Textile banner, by unknown artist, [1801]. Size: 30 x 37 in. Drawing of Jefferson, embellished by stars and an eagle holding streamers inscribed: "T. Jefferson, President of the United States of America" and "John Adams is no More." National Museum of History and Technology, Smithsonian Institution. Fig. 60

54. Thomas Jefferson. Portrait on glass, engraved in gold by A. B. Doolittle, 1803. Size: 3 ½ x 3 in. Thomas Jefferson Memorial Foundation, Monticello. Fig. 59

Note on Sources

ENGRAVED PRINTS OF JEFFERSON CONTEMPORANEOUS with his presidency are widely scattered. The best collections are those of the Thomas Jefferson Memorial Foundation at Monticello, the William J. Campbell Collection at the American Philosophical Society, the Mabel Brady Garvan Collection at the Yale University Art Gallery, and collections at the Metropolitan Museum of Art, the New York Public Library, and the University of Virginia. There are also valuable prints at the Atwater Kent Museum, Boston Museum of Fine Arts, Essex Institute, Historical Society of Pennsylvania, Library of Congress, Massachusetts Historical Society, National Portrait Gallery of the Smithsonian Institution, Princeton University, and Virginia Historical Society. The best prints of Jefferson in caricature are in the Houghton Library, Harvard University.

The best collections of Liverpool earthenware with Jefferson's image are in the National Museum of History and Technology of the Smithsonian Institution and the Peabody Museum of Salem.

The most useful manuscript sources are the Mathew Carey letter books in the Lea and Febiger Collection, Historical Society of Pennsylvania; Mathew Carey account books in the American Antiquarian Society; Peale Papers and Peale-Sellers Papers in the American Philosophical Society; Thomas Jefferson Papers, Library of Congress; Jefferson Papers, Coolidge Collection, Massachusetts Historical Society; and Jefferson Papers, Harold Jefferson Coolidge Collection, University of Virginia.

Advertisements in newspapers have been especially useful in indicating the sale of prints of Jefferson to the public. The Philadelphia *Aurora* has been the most valuable source in this respect, but numerous other newspapers, as cited in the footnotes, published useful notices. Valuable sources for newspaper advertisements also are Rita Susswein Gottesman, *The Arts and Crafts in New York, 1779–1799: Advertisements and News Items from New York City Newspapers* (New York, 1954), and *The Arts and Crafts in New York, 1800–1804: Advertisements and News Items from New York City Newspapers* (New York, 1965); and Alfred Coxe Prime, ed., *The Arts and Crafts in Philadelphia, Maryland, and South Carolina, 1786–1800: Gleanings from Newspapers* (The Walpole Society, 1932).

The most authoritative work on Jefferson portraiture is Alfred L. Bush, *The Life Portraits of Thomas Jefferson: Catalogue of an Exhibition at the University of Virginia Museum of Fine Arts, 12 through 26 April 1962* (Charlottesville, Va., 1962); a revised edition, "The Life Portraits of Thomas Jefferson," has been published in William Howard Adams, ed., *Jefferson and the Arts: An Extended View* (Washington, D.C., 1976). Bush's work builds on Fiske Kimball, "The Life Portraits of Jefferson and Their Replicas," American Philosophical Society, *Proceedings* 88 (1944): 497–534, which is still a basic work. Kimball's work superseded Charles Henry Hart, "Life Portraits of Thomas Jefferson, *McClure's Magazine* 11 (1898): 47–55. Also important is William Howard Adams, ed., *The Eye of Thomas Jefferson* (Washington, D.C., 1976), the superb catalogue of the National Gallery of Art Bicentennial Exhibition.

Note on Sources

Although it does not list all of the American prints identified in this study, the most complete catalogue of American engravings is David McNeely Stauffer, *American Engravers upon Copper and Steel*, 2 vols. (New York, 1907), supplemented by Mantle Fielding, *American Engravers upon Copper and Steel* (Philadelphia, 1917). Stauffer and Fielding did not attempt to date the prints listed. The following sales catalogues have also been useful in identifying engravings: Stanislaus V. Henkels, comp., *The Unique [Hampton L. Carson] Collection of Engraved Portraits of Thomas Jefferson, Benjamin Franklin, and Gilbert Mottier de La Fayette* (Philadelphia, [1904]), and Henkels, *The Unequalled Collection of Engraved Portraits of the Presidents of the United States Belonging to Hon. James T. Mitchell* (Philadelphia, 1907). Also useful is Boston Museum of Fine Arts, *A Descriptive Catalogue of an Exhibition of Early Engraving in America, December 12, 1904–February 5, 1905* (Cambridge, Mass., 1904).

Engravers in early America have not received much attention, but some of them were noticed in William Dunlap, *A History of the Rise and Progress of the Arts of Design in the United States*, ed. Frank W. Bayley and Charles E. Goodspeed, 3 vols. (Boston, 1918), first published in 1834. Wendy J. Shadwell, *American Printmaking: The First 150 Years* (Washington, D.C., 1969), contains the most extensive collection of important early American prints reproduced in a single work, though only one print of Jefferson is included. Useful background can be found in Joan D. Dolmetsch, ed., *Eighteenth Century Prints in Colonial America* (Charlottesville, Va., 1979). Saint-Mémin has received considerable attention in Elias Dexter, *The St.-Mémin Collection of Portraits; Consisting of Seven Hundred and Sixty Medallion Portraits, Principally of Distinguished Americans* (New York, 1862), and Fillmore Norfleet, *Saint-Mémin in Virginia: Portraits and Biographies* (Richmond, 1942). Particularly pertinent to this study is the scholarly article by Howard C. Rice, Jr., "Saint-Mémin's Portrait of Jefferson," *Princeton University Library Chronicle* 20 (1959): 182–92.

For portraits appearing on Liverpool earthenware the major studies are Robert H. McCauley, *Liverpool Transfer Designs on Anglo-American Pottery* (Portland, Me., 1942), and Alan Smith, *The Illustrated Guide to Liverpool Herculaneum Pottery, 1796–1840* (New York, 1970).

For images on Indian peace medals, Francis Paul Prucha, *Indian Peace Medals in American History* (Madison, Wis., 1971) is indispensable; also important is Bauman L. Belden, *Indian Peace Medals Issued in the United States* (New Milford, Conn., 1966).

The principal works that include some treatment of early American caricatures are Frank Weitenkampf, *Political Caricature in the United States in Separately Published Cartoons* (New York, 1953), an annotated list; William Murrell, *A History of American Graphic Humor*, 2 vols. (New York, 1933–38); and Thomas C. Blaisdell, Jr., Peter Selz, et al., *The American Presidency in Political Cartoons: 1776–1976* (Berkeley, Calif., 1976). See also *Made in America, Printmaking 1760–1860: An Exhibition of Original Prints from the Collections of the Library Company of Philadelphia and the Historical Society of Pennsylvania, April-June, 1973* (Philadelphia, 1973).

On silhouettees see *The Monticello Family: Catalogue of an Exhibition Held at the University of Virginia Museum of Fine Arts, April 12–May 13, 1960* (Charlottesville, Va., 1960), and Alice Van Leer Carrick, *Shades of Our Ancestors: American Profiles and Profilists* (Boston, 1928).

Extremely important work on early American portraiture and iconography has been done by Andrew Oliver in three studies: *Portraits of John and Abigail Adams* (Cambridge, Mass., 1967); *Portraits of John Quincy Adams and His Wife* (Cambridge, Mass., 1970); and *The Portraits of John Marshall* (Charlottesville, Va., 1977). Of these, the volume on John and Abigail Adams has been especially helpful. Also useful are Charles Coleman Sellers, *Benjamin Franklin in Portraiture* (New Haven, 1962), and Marvin S. Sadik, *Colonial and Federal Portraits at Bowdoin College* (Brunswick, Me., 1966).

Note on Sources

Among studies of early American artists the most useful have been the works by Charles Coleman Sellers: *Charles Willson Peale*, 2 vols. (Philadelphia, 1947), and *Portraits and Miniatures of Charles Willson Peale* (Philadelphia, 1952). Also important are Harry Piers, *Robert Field: Portrait Painter in Oils, Miniature, and Water-Colours and Engraver* (New York, 1927); William T. Whitley, *Gilbert Stuart* (Cambridge, Mass., 1932); Charles Merrill Mount, *Gilbert Stuart, a Biography* (New York, 1964); and Lawrence Park, *Gilbert Stuart: An Illustrated Descriptive List of His Works*, 4 vols. (New York, 1926).

The best bibliography of works relating to early American prints is *Prints Pertaining to America: A List of Publications in English, Relating to Prints about That Portion of America Now Included in the United States with Emphasis on the Period 1650–1850, and a Checklist of Prints in an Exhibition to Commemorate the 1962 Fall Meeting of the Walpole Society Selected from the Collection of the Henry Francis DuPont Winterthur Museum* (The Walpole Society, 1963).

Appendix

Sources of the People's Image

Pl. I. Bust of Jefferson by Jean-Antoine Houdon, 1789. Plaster original given by Jefferson to David Rittenhouse in 1793 and presented by his daughter to the American Philosophical Society in 1811

Pl. II. Oil portrait of Jefferson taken from life by Charles Willson Peale in 1791 and publicly displayed in Peale's Museum in Philadelphia. Now in Independence National Historical Park Collection, Philadelphia

Pl. III. Crayon profile of Jefferson by James Sharples, drawn in 1797. Now in Independence National Historical Park Collection, Philadelphia

Pl. IV. Oil portrait of Jefferson taken from life by Rembrandt Peale in 1800. Now in the White House

Pl. V. Crayon drawing of Jefferson taken from life in 1804 by Charles-Balthazar-Julien Févret de Saint-Mémin. Now at the Worcester Art Museum

Pl. VI. Oil portrait of Jefferson painted by Gilbert Stuart for James Bowdoin III, begun in 1805 and completed in 1807. Now at the Bowdoin College Museum of Art

Pl. VII. "Medallion" profile of Jefferson by Gilbert Stuart, 1805. Now at the Fogg Art Museum, Harvard University

Pl. VIII. Oil portrait of Jefferson painted by Rembrandt Peale in 1805. Now at the New-York Historical Society

Credits

Figure

1. Atwater Kent Museum, Philadelphia.
2. The Metropolitan Museum of Art. Bequest of Charles Allen Munn, 1924.
3. The Metropolitan Museum of Art. Bequest of Charles Allen Munn, 1924.
4. Noble E. Cunningham, Jr.
5. Noble E. Cunningham, Jr.
6. Rare Book Division, Library of Congress.
7. Museum of Fine Arts, Boston.
8. Yale University Art Gallery, Mabel Brady Garvan Collection.
9. Yale University Art Gallery, Mabel Brady Garvan Collection.
10. Emmet Collection no. 1371, Manuscripts and Archives Division, The New York Public Library, Astor, Lenox and Tilden Foundations.
11. Emmet Collection no. 10226, Manuscripts and Archives Division, The New York Public Library, Astor, Lenox and Tilden Foundations.
12. Virginia State Library, Richmond.
13. Rare Book Division, Library of Congress.
14. Yale University Art Gallery, Mabel Brady Garvan Collection.

15. Noble E. Cunningham, Jr.
16. Rare Book Division, The New York Public Library, Astor, Lenox and Tilden Foundations.
17. Massachusetts Historical Society, Boston.
18. Virginia State Library, Richmond.
19. Library of Congress.
20. William J. Campbell Collection, American Philosophical Society, Philadelphia.
21. General Research and Humanities Division, The New York Public Library, Astor, Lenox and Tilden Foundations.
22. Manuscripts Department, University of Virginia Library.
23. Manuscripts Department, University of Virginia Library.
24. General Research and Humanities Division, The New York Public Library, Astor, Lenox and Tilden Foundations.
25. National Portrait Gallery, Smithsonian Institution, Washington, D. C.
26. Noble E. Cunningham, Jr.
27. Emmet Collection no. 2529, Manuscripts and Archives Division, The New York Public Library, Astor, Lenox and Tilden Foundations.
28. Virginia Historical Society, Richmond.
29. Historical Society of Pennsylvania, Philadelphia.
30. Library of Congress.
31. American Numismatic Society, New York.
32. American Numismatic Society, New York.
33. American Numismatic Society, New York.
34. American Numismatic Society, New York.
35. Harold Jefferson Coolidge, Jefferson Papers, Coolidge Collection, University of Virginia Library.

36. Rare Book Room, Princeton University Library.
37. William J. Campbell Collection, American Philosophical Society.
38. The Metropolitan Museum of Art. Bequest of Charles Allen Munn, 1924.
39. Manuscripts Department, University of Virginia Library.
40. National Museum of History and Technology, Smithsonian Institution (photo no. 77–4126).
41. National Museum of History and Technology, Smithsonian Institution (photo no. 77–4125).
42. City of Manchester Art Galleries, Thomas Greg Collection.
43. Peabody Museum of Salem, Massachusetts.
44. National Museum of History and Technology, Smithsonian Institution (photo no. 49455A).
45. Peabody Museum of Salem, Massachusetts.
46. National Museum of History and Technology, Smithsonian Institution (photo no. 77–4124).
47. Alan Smith, Manchester, England.
48. Dedham Historical Society, Dedham, Massachusetts.
49. National Museum of History and Technology, Smithsonian Institution (photo no. 77–4127).
50. National Museum of History and Technology, Smithsonian Institution (photo no. 58991A).
51. National Museum of History and Technology, Smithsonian Institution (photo no. 77–4128).
52. The New-York Historical Society, New York.
53. Thomas Jefferson Memorial Foundation, Monticello.
54. The Free Library of Philadelphia.
55. The Houghton Library, Harvard University.
56. The Houghton Library, Harvard University.

57. Thomas Jefferson Memorial Foundation, Monticello.
58. Kirby Collection of Historical Paintings, Lafayette College, Easton, Pennsylvania.
59. Thomas Jefferson Memorial Foundation, Monticello.
60. National Museum of History and Technology, Smithsonian Institution (photo no. 45553).

Plate I. American Philosophical Society, Philadelphia.

II. Independence National Historical Park Collection, Philadelphia.

III. Independence National Historical Park Collection, Philadelphia.

IV. White House Collection, The White House, Washington, D.C.

V. Worcester Art Museum, Worcester, Massachusetts.

VI. Bowdoin College Museum of Art, Brunswick, Maine.

VII. Fogg Art Museum, Harvard University.

VIII. The New-York Historical Society, New York.

Index

Index